CHRISTIAN COMMUNITY:
BIBLICAL OR OPTIONAL?

Christian Community: Biblical or Optional?

Hal Miller

SERVANT BOOKS
Ann Arbor, Michigan

Published by: Servant Publications
            Box 8617
            Ann Arbor, Michigan 48107

Printed in the United States of America

ISBN 0-89283-068-9

*For Dianne
and for Ray*

ACKNOWLEDGEMENTS

It would probably take another book at least as long as this one to thank all the people to whom I am indebted. This book has been a community effort from the beginning, and would never have been completed if not for the contributions and encouragement of dozens of people. Their work has been so essential to the birth of this book that although I must take responsibility for what is here, I could never take credit for all of it. So, as a hopelessly insufficient installment on my debt, I would like to thank the following people specifically.

Two men who have influenced my thought, life, and person beyond measure: Francis A. Schaeffer (whom I have never met) and Ray Nethery.

My chief encouragers: Peter and Alison Spellman, Danny Meyer, John Cook, Kevin Springer, Frank Jernigan, and Craig Schoelles.

Those who have shared with me in the mundane tasks of typing, indexing, correcting my (horrible) spelling, and the like: especially Paula Stevenson and Glyn Jones Rhodes.

And my wife, who has done all the above, and more.

CONTENTS

INTRODUCTION

By Howard A. Snyder

Christian Community: Biblical or Optional? is an important contribution to the current discussion about the future direction of the church. Hal Miller creatively combines Evangelical and Charismatic concerns in calling for an experience of the church which takes seriously biblical teachings about Christian community. More basically, Miller is faithful to scripture in showing what the true nature of Christian community is.

According to Miller, the "great error of the modern church" is, very simply, its lack of community. Orthodoxy has not been tied to orthopraxy — right belief to right practice — in much of the contemporary church. For too many of us, Christian community is seen as optional only, not as something essential to biblical faithfulness. But a church without community is a church without power — not merely for sociological reasons, but for fundamental spiritual reasons having to do with our creation in the image of God.

Miller argues that in God's plan "the word of God to be proclaimed is to be accompanied by the image of God to be displayed in the world." Salvation is God's work of restoring the image of God among his children — not merely as the inward experience of individual believers, but as the building of renewed communities which truly become the Body of Christ and grow into the fullness of the image of Jesus.

It is a sure biblical instinct which leads the author to stress the image of God. To talk about the Word of God without stressing the image of God is to narrow the focus of God's revelation and to fall prey to an unbiblical biblicism. For the Word which was made flesh and tabernacled among us is none other than "the image of the invisible God, the firstborn over all creation" (Col

1

1:15); "the radiance of God's glory and the exact representation of his being" (Heb 1:3). And God's purpose for the church is that we be conformed not to the world but to "the image of his Son" (Rom 8:29).

Luther and other reformers stressed the Word of God. *Sola Scriptura* — God's Word operating by grace through faith — was the rallying cry of the Reformation. But an element was missing — an element which had to do with Christian community and the shape of the church. Sixty years after Luther's death, a Lutheran pastor named John Arndt published *True Christianity*, a book that helped spark renewal among Lutherans and Anglicans and which circulated in some Roman Catholic orders. The book concerns "the whole economy of God toward Man; and the whole duty of Man toward God," and its starting point is the image of God. According to Arndt, true Christians not only repent and believe in Jesus Christ for salvation; they also imitate their Master and seek the restoration of his image in their lives and relationships.

It was an introduction to Arndt's *True Christianity* by Philipp Jakob Spener, published in 1675 (Spener's *Pia Desideria*) which launched the Pietiest Movement in Germany, with its practice of small house fellowships for Bible study and prayer. From this movement in part grew the Moravian Brethern with their small, intense missionary communities which spread to three continents. And *True Christianity* was a favorite book of John Wesley, whose Methodist cells and societies within the eighteenth century church of England led thousands of Anglicans not only to Christ but to Christian community as well.

John Wesley never tired of describing salvation in terms of the restoration of the image of God in believers. To him, true Christianity was "the life of God in the soul of man; a participation of the divine nature; the mind that was in Christ; or, the renewal of our heart after the image of Him that created us." But the image of God is not a narrow or sectarian concern. Like the experience of Christian community itself, the theme of the image of God is a renewing thread running down through the centuries of Christian history. From early monasticism to the present day, the biblical ideal of recovering God's image in present life and experience has sparked renewal and, often, renewed Christian community in the life of the church.

Hal Miller's point is that our re-creation in God's image is not simply an internal spiritual reality, nor merely a matter of our vertical relationship to God. It concerns the horizontal. It is the body of Christ, the church, which is to bear and express God's image. And this means some form of genuine Christian community is, for all of us, not optional but essential. To the extent we do not experience the kind of Christian *koinonia* depicted in the New Testament, to that extent we are simply not Christians.

Miller is right, and this is a timely word. His book sparkles with bright new insights the church desperately needs today. Here is a vision of the church that is at once evangelical, catholic, and charismatic.

Let us then get on with building the Christian community, renewed after the image of God, so that God's glory and reconciliation will be revealed not only in the church but throughout God's whole universe — so that his Kingdom may come on earth, as well as in heaven.

Christian Community:
God's People And God's Image

CHRISTIAN COMMUNITY: GOD'S PEOPLE AND GOD'S IMAGE

WE live in a world that our great-grandparents never would have recognized. Instant communication, rapid transportation, and indoor plumbing — things which we take for granted each day — were unheard of until a little over a century ago. During the last hundred years, the face of the earth and the life of man have been drastically altered by the force of technology. This child of modern science has revolutionized our world.

Of course, technology has not only brought us benefits; it has brought us difficulty as well. We hardly need look beyond the delicate balancing act of the nuclear superpowers to see that our scientific wisdom has been at best a mixed blessing. The technology of atomic energy, which might be used for great good, can also be used to produce unimaginable destruction. Yet, in spite of this basic ambivalence of technology, most people today still see it as something of a "savior." Modern man, if he believes in anything, believes that science and technology will eventually solve all his problems.

In this climate of belief in technology as man's savior, there has been much talk about the survival of Christianity. Can the church survive, let alone grow and prosper, in a technological era? Can people still believe in a God who acts supernaturally in history when the final test of all truth is verification by the scientific method? Is a God who authors miracles "out of date" in an age when miracles are thought to be things of the past?

And what of preaching the good news? Can Christians still speak of God who is really there, who transforms lives by a new birth, who works sovereignly in the created order? Does the church dare to preach such a gospel to a world which acknowledges no truth but the mechanistic laws of nature?

How can the church speak in such a time?

Questions like these are being asked partly because our models of the way the church speaks are inadequate. When I think of preaching the good news, the image that comes to my mind is that of a somewhat sober-looking gentleman, standing on a platform, Bible in hand, speaking of the life and death of Jesus and calling the people around him to repent. It is good that this image, and ones like it, are the primary content of our understanding of speaking the good news. The preaching ministry of the church is a vastly important part of her way of proclaiming the gospel. But is preaching all there is to it?

Paul's words on love are seldom applied to speaking the good news, but they are nevertheless important if we want to understand how the people of God are the bearers of good news.

> If I speak in the tongues of men and of angels, but have not love, I am a noisy gong or a clanging cymbal. And if I have prophetic powers, and understand all mysteries and all knowledge, and if I have all faith, so as to remove mountains, but have not love, I am nothing. (1 Cor 13:1-2)

Paul says that one can speak as beautifully as angels and possess great knowledge of God and his mysteries, and yet be worthless. The missing element? Love. Without love, all the preaching in the world is just noise.

But in the biblical understanding, love is not just a matter of attitudes; it is a matter of actions as well. When John says, "Dear children, let us not love with words or tongue but *with actions and in truth*" (1 Jn 3:18) he makes it plain that a loving attitude divorced from loving actions is inadequate. The love which must go with the church's speaking of the good news is a love which is expressed concretely.

Speaking and Loving

Most of the models we have inherited for sharing the good news have failed to integrate the actions of love with the preaching of the gospel. My own image of the man preaching from a platform tends to isolate the communication of the gospel's content from the love which must accompany it. How can this gentleman act out of love toward those who hear him? If, when we consider proclamation of the gospel, we mean nothing more than speakers saying words to listeners, the most our man on the platform can do is "speak with the tongues of men and angels." He can *say* he is acting out love, but he is hardly in a position to *do* it.

Such models of speaking the gospel are the ones used by virtually the entire evangelical church. Mere speaking, however, even if it is with the tongues of angels, is not all that the proclamation of the gospel involves. Even though this kind of preaching by speaking only is very common, we should consider two objections to its validity.

1. *It is not the biblical model.*

Preaching the good news is something which happens over and over again in the Gospels and in Acts, but it is not preaching as we tend to think of it. Jesus came to preach (Mk 1:38), but Mark's summary of his preaching is, "And he went throughout all Galilee, preaching in their synagogues *and casting out demons*" (Mk 1:39). Jesus' preaching was not just in words, but was in words accompanied by concrete acts of love—in this case casting out demons.

Matthew confirms that this was Jesus' way. His message was, "Repent, for the kingdom of heaven is at hand" (Mt 4:17), but this was expressed by "preaching the gospel of the kingdom and healing every disease and every infirmity among the people" (Mt 4:23). Here again, Jesus' preaching was always accompanied by concrete loving acts like healings. Even when John the Baptist sent some of his disciples to ask Jesus whether he was really the Messiah, Jesus' response contained both these elements. Jesus told them, "Go and tell John what you *hear and see*: the blind receive their sight and the lame walk, lepers are cleansed and the deaf hear, and the dead are raised up, *and* the poor have good news preached to them" (Mt 11:4-5). Jesus did not tell John's disciples to just report what they heard, but what they heard *and saw*. *Hearing* the good news and *seeing* actions of love are inseparable in Jesus' ministry.

In the book of Acts, preaching is accompanied by acts of love, but the focus of those acts of love changes. The sphere of God's loving action is not just in miracles, but also in the miracle of the loving Christian community. Healings and other miracles are still associated with the apostolic preaching (see Acts 3:1-4:4), but the focus in general has shifted from the loving acts of an individual preacher to the life of love of the church. Look, for example, at the way preaching is sandwiched between descriptions of the loving community in this portrayal of the situation in Jerusalem:

Now the company of those who believed were of one heart and soul, and no one said that any of the things which he possessed was his own, but they had everything in common. *And with great power the apostles gave their testimony to the resurrection of the Lord Jesus*, and great grace was upon them all. There was not a needy person among them. (Acts 4:32-34)

Clearly, loving actions and preaching the good news of Christ are inseparable in the Gospels and in Acts. In the apostolic church, proclamation of the good news was carried out in the context of a community of Christians who were acting out love for one another. By isolating preaching as an end in itself, we have violated this biblical pattern of "speaking the truth *in love.*"

2. *Simply preaching the gospel is not an effective method because it sells the message short.*

Not only is the separation of preaching from acting love unbiblical, but it is also less effective than when preaching and loving actions are combined. We live in a pluralistic culture, in which dozens of alternate philosophies and world views compete for people's minds. Transcendental Meditation, existentialism, materialism, Marxism, and Christianity are only a few of the options before contemporary man. A Christian cannot say that these are all equally valid belief systems. In contrast to the old liberal idea that the many religions are different ways to the one God,

Jesus says, "I am the way, and the truth, and the life; no one comes to the Father, but by me" (Jn 14:6). Christianity can be tolerant of other religions and philosophies; after all, a person has the right to be wrong if he so chooses. However, Christians cannot say that they are equally valid ways of knowing the truth.

If Christianity says that it stands alone among the various philosophies and religions as the one true way, what can it offer to support this assertion? Why would anyone believe such a claim? Does Christianity offer a rationally consistent system of thought? Many philosophers from Plato on offer that. Does it offer personal fulfillment? Modern affluent materialism claims to give that. Does it offer social change? So does Marxism. What evidence does Christianity offer in support of its claim? Or to put it another way, how is Christianity to be validated?

There are two answers to this question: a comprehensive one and a concrete one. The comprehensive answer is that Christianity is validated by the sovereign action of God in the heart and mind of man. Scripture says that "the Spirit himself bears witness with our spirit that we are children of God" (Rom 8:16). Ultimately, the validation of Christianity rests not in its logical consistency or promise of meaningful life, but in the testimony of the Holy Spirit that these things are really true. It is ultimately God alone who convicts people of their sin and brings them to repentance and faith, even though "the word of the cross is folly to those who are perishing" (1 Cor 1:18). God does this so that our salvation can be based on his grace and not on our intelligence or goodness.

But, having said this, we are still faced with the question, "how is Christianity validated?" Even though we know that God acts sovereignly to bring about our salvation, we also know that he doesn't bypass our humanity when he does so. The testimony of the Holy Spirit to the truth of our salvation is not a flash from outer space. God does not just "zap" us so that we believe in contradiction to everything else that touches us. Rather, God works through the things around us, testifying to us in concrete actions. After all, no one has ever listened to the gospel and said, "That's the stupidest thing I've ever heard; I think I'll believe it." How then does God validate the message of the cross *concretely*?

This brings us to the second answer to our question of validation: God also validates the gospel by *his visible acts of love* which are coordinated with preaching. The book of Hebrews puts it like this: When the apostles preached the good news, "God also bore witness by signs and wonders and various miracles" (Heb 2:4). As we have seen in the ministry of Jesus and the apostolic church, these acts of love given by God to accompany the preaching of the gospel are an external witness to the truth of the good news.

Of course, no one is ever saved by signs and wonders. Though Jesus performed many miracles, he rebuked people for concentrating only on these external witnesses instead of on his person and message (Mt 12:38-39). God's concrete testimony to the truth of the gospel is external, and it is secondary to the gospel itself. Nonetheless, these loving acts of God are always to be correlated with preaching. They are inescapable partners of biblical proclamation.

As we seek to coordinate preaching with acting love, our model should be that of the apostolic church. There, this external testimony of love was given not so much through certain miraculous signs performed by an individual preacher as it was through the loving life of the Christian church itself. Jesus himself emphasized that this was a proper shift in focus when he prayed for those who would believe in him: "That they may become perfectly one [that is, live a life of concrete love with each other], *so the world may know that thou hast sent me* and hast loved them even as thou hast loved me" (Jn 17:23). The loving life of the church is to be a witness to the truth of the good news that the Son of God has come into the world.

This is especially important for us as we seek to be faithful to the Lord in the twentieth century. Our age is one of skepticism, one which refuses to believe anything which it cannot test with its senses. It is, as we noted earlier, an age where the final test of truth is verification by the scientific method. This method is empirical: It takes sense observations and tries to fit them into a pattern. Yet because the scientific method can deal only with sense information, it is not applicable to the non-material being of God. Thus it is inappropriate as an ultimate test of Christianity.

Nonetheless, Jesus has given man the privilege of asking for a secondary, empirical test of the truth of Christianity. This test is the concrete reality of the loving life of the people of God, for the empirical way God testifies to the reality of the spoken message is by acts of love. We live in an age which "asks for a sign" that Jesus Christ really came from the Father. The sign that God has ordained is not found in logical consistency or social change (as important as these may be) but in the act of God which brings about love in the Christian community. This is the inescapable companion to the preaching of the gospel. If we preach the gospel without this companion — the loving life of the Christian community — we are denying people the test of Christianity's truth which Jesus gave to them. Without this concrete validation, our method of preaching is both unbiblical and ineffective because we are giving people only part of what they ought to have to see the truth of the good news.

Image of God and Proclamation

As we begin to consider Christian community, we must see that it is by nature two-fold. First, it is *Christian* community. It is based on the relationship God's people have with him through Christ. Second, it is Christian *community*. It manifests itself in loving personal relationships among those who call God their Father. In Christian community, the children of God are called to live as brothers and sisters to one another.

There has been much discussion in recent years about Christian community. Some say it is just another fad. Others say it is central to the Christian life. If we are going to reach a proper understanding of Christian community, especially as it relates to our preaching of the Gospel, the question we must answer is: Is Christian community biblical, or is it optional?

Unfortunately, answering this question is not a simple matter. It would be nice if we could just collect a bouquet of proof texts and leave it at that. But we cannot merely do this. We also need to see how the practice of Christian community is related to other great teachings of scripture. How is it related to the nature of man, for instance? Or to the church? Unless we can relate Christian community to the broader teaching of the scriptures, we cannot say that it is "biblical" in the true sense.

Because Christian community must be related to the other teachings of scripture, we must take a seemingly roundabout way of answering our question: Is Christian community biblical or optional? We need to start with our nature as the image bearers of God. Believers are called to reflect something of God's nature to the world around them (Rom 8:29; 1 Cor 11:7; Eph 4:24; and others). We do not reflect God's image perfectly, for we are fallen, damaged creatures. Yet even in our fallen state we are to act as clouded mirrors, reflecting a true, even if indistinct, image of the God we worship.

As we will see, the Christian's role as the image bearer of God finds expression in loving relationships with God and with other Christians. The witness of loving life which must accompany our preaching of the gospel is, in fact, summarized in the concept of bearing God's image. When we act as the bearers of God's image, we witness to the truth of the gospel by demonstrating in a life of love that Jesus Christ really was sent into the world by the Father. The Word of God which is to be proclaimed to all men is to be accompanied by the image of God which is to be displayed in the world in a concrete life of love. This life gives visible confirmation to the message.

To understand how Christians are to act as bearers of God's image, we will have to answer two basic questions. The first is: What does it mean that man is created in the image and likeness of God? This question will occupy us in the first two chapters, and we will find that man was created in God's image to have loving fellowship with both God and other men. The second question is: How does the church—the community of believers—reflect the image of God? We will look at this question in Chapters Three through Five. There we will see how bearing God's image works out into the loving life of the church as a concrete testimony to the truth of the gospel.

It is important to keep in mind that God's desire for us is to integrate our thought with our actions. Although we will examine much scripture and try to form a base of concepts concerning the image of God, ultimately the goal is that this conceptual base be translated into practical forms of life. Only when these concepts are worked into our lives in a lifestyle of love will our role as clouded mirrors reflecting the image of God have the place which it must in our proclamation of the gospel. Only then can we point to the church and say, "Look, here is a concrete example of God's loving action. This is a living confirmation of the gospel we preach."

Part One

The Basis of Christian Community

ONE

CREATION AND COMMUNITY: THE FALLEN IMAGE

Not long ago, we witnessed one of the great technological marvels of our time — the first so-called "test tube baby." A woman in England gave birth to a child which had been conceived outside her womb, and then reimplanted in her uterus. Apparently this was a great blessing to the parents who otherwise would not have been able to have a child of their own. Even though such a procedure is a long way from "creating life" as some of the popular press claimed (it was actually just a chemical duplication of the environment and mechanics of a mother's womb) this should not cause us to underrate the complexity and genius of the feat. It was a great technical achievement.

The problem with this technical accomplishment is that it was apparently carried out without a thorough consideration of the moral and ethical issues involved. Unfortunately, this is our standard procedure in dealing with technological advances: we do the thing first, and *then* ask questions. We make a nuclear bomb and *then* face its grim implications for the world. We build huge industrial complexes and *then* face the pollution which these complexes produce. We conceive a child in a "test tube" and *then* ask if it's good.

Now it may well turn out that the conception of children outside the mother's womb is a good thing. That's not the point. The point is that we never seem to consider the possibility of voluntarily limiting our technical curiosity because of the social impact it might have. We insist on doing the thing first — whether it be building the Bomb or conceiving a "test tube" baby—and *then* worrying about its ethical implications. Following our technical noses blindly until it's too late to turn back is surely the path into Huxley's "brave new world."

We might face the same issue anew if it becomes possible to "clone" human beings. Science fiction writers are no longer the only people who think that it may be just a matter of time until we can make hundreds of identical human beings by processing the information from genetic material. The prospect is perversely fascinating: Imagine little men in white coats scurrying around, working feverishly to make a thousand Beethovens or a thousand Einsteins. Or will they be making a thousand thousand storm troopers to hold the human race in bondage?

Who will decide whether to make great composers or smoothly efficient soldiers? It's frightening to think of that kind of power in the hands of a few. And what will it mean to be a "person" when there are dozens of others just like you? "I've got to be me," says the song, but what does "me" mean? If we do learn to produce human clones, the person will become utterly depersonalized.

Of course, those fateful experiments may never be carried out. Maybe some insurmountable difficulties will keep a "brave new world" from becoming our reality. We may even learn to limit ourselves when we cannot predict the social cost of technical advance. But even if human clones never come into being, the fact of human depersonalization which cloning raises so dramatically would still be with us. Even now our culture can be aptly described as "depersonalized." The person is being viewed less and less as a unique creation of God, and more and more as a series of numbers which can be punched on an IBM card. Our newest technological servant, the computer, is rapidly remaking us in its own image.

Time magazine has called this "The Computer Society," a label which is a good deal more profound than it appears at first glance. Not only do information processing machines play an ever-larger role in our lives, but we are becoming more and more computer-like ourselves. The ideal businessman, bureaucrat, or politician needs to be cool, efficient, unemotional, and totally identified with his work—just like a computer. It's as if our kinship is no longer greatest with the "unenlightened" human beings who lived before us, but instead with the machines which surround us. In a real way we look to our machines rather than to our ancestors for models of life.

When we begin to find our closest identity with machines rather than people, is it any wonder that the question which arises for us again and again is: Who am I? We no longer know what it means to be human. Our whole culture seems to be going through a long "identity crisis." When we consider genetic experiments like cloning, the question underneath it is: What is man? When we consider abortion on demand, the question underneath it is: What is man? When we consider the issue of maintaining comatose patients on respirators, the question underneath it is: What is man?

Asking the Right Question

Yet the question "what is man?" is by no means a new one. Listen to the words of the psalmist:

> When I look at the heavens, the work of thy fingers
>   the moon and the stars which thou hast established;
> what is man that thou art mindful of him,
>   and the son of man that thou dost care for him?
> Yet thou hast made him little less than God,
>   and dost crown him with glory and honor.
> Thou hast given him dominion over the works of thy hands;
>   thou hast put all things under his feet. (Ps 8:3-6)

Did you notice the subtle difference between the way we ask the question "what is man?" and the way the psalmist asks it? When we ask "what is man?" that's all we say. We try in vain to reach out beyond ourselves for something, anything, to give meaning to our lives. We try to transcend ourselves by saying that we are reasonable beings, or that we produce art, or that we use tools, or some such thing. The problem is that none of the things we grasp at can finally make sense out of our humanity. And the reason for this problem is that we've asked the wrong question.

The psalmist poses a different question. He does not simply ask what is man? but, what is man *that thou art mindful of him*? The psalmist is not interested in man's nature in itself; he wants to know about man as God relates to him. If we want to discover who we are by trying to transcend ourselves, we will be frustrated. There is no good answer to the question "what is man?" when it is asked by itself, without being followed by "that thou art mindful of him."

One reason why there is no good answer to the simple question "what is man?" divorced from God's perspective is that man seems to be a bundle of contradictions. For example, some people have thought that man's uniqueness lies in his rationality. No doubt man's rational processes make him unique, but a glance at history will tell you that man is irrational just about as much as he is rational.

The contradictions go even deeper than rational man's repeated irrationality. One of the basic drives within every human being is an ultimately selfish desire for his own preservation. Yet many people are willing to give their lives in support of a cause, or to save another person's life. This kind of selflessness stands in stark contrast to man's otherwise selfish behavior.

Overall, there is much that is good in what man does: His art, music, and the cleverness of his inventions show the genius and beauty which is his. Yet the unspeakable evil man perpetrates—the wars and oppression and violence—do not allow us realistically to consider man to be "good." In his goodness and his evil, man is a contradiction to himself. In each individual, and in every group of people, we see exhibited both the divine aspects of man and the demonic.

We will be frustrated by the contradictions of our nature unless we are willing to ask the psalmist's question: What is man that Thou art mindful of him? God considers these contradictions in man to be basic to who he is. They are not just a passing phase. We will not grow out of our irrational rationality as our evolution continues; rather, these contradictions run to the core of our beings. Man does good and brings forth beautiful things because he was created as the image bearer of God. He does evil as well because he is hopelessly damaged. Man is no longer as God created him.

Man resembles a car that some drunken driver has wrapped around a tree. The car was a thing of beauty when it was made. It was useful for carrying people and things. But now it is smashed beyond recognition. The radio may still play; the engine may still run, coughing and sputtering. But the car no longer fulfills the purpose for which it was built.

The same kind of thing has happened to man: He was created a thing of elegance and beauty, but now he is wrecked. He is still man, but he is horribly damaged. When we look at ourselves after the damage has been done, these contradictions are very apparent. No wonder man is a mystery to himself.

This dilemma of man's nature is laid out clearly in the Genesis account of man's creation and fall. Man was created as the bearer of God's image, the glorious center of the creation, but he fell into rebellion and brought about his own destruction. The story of man's creation and fall tells of both his glory and his tragedy.

And through this story we will be able to take the first steps toward understanding the biblical basis of Christian community.

Man: The Climax of Creation

The first chapter of Genesis is marked by a sense of sweeping grandeur. "In the beginning, God created the heavens and the earth" (Gn 1:1). Here we are immediately confronted with God's unimaginable power: Nothing in the vastness of the universe can compare with him, for he is the One who brought it into being from nothing. The creation story does not picture God as a disinterested power, but as an artist at work on his masterpiece. Genesis shows God's power and his loving sensitivity each time he steps back and pronounces a part of his creation "good." C.S. Lewis captured this loving power by portraying God "singing" his creation into being as if he were a masterful composer creating a symphony.

The focus of the Genesis narrative is not on the vast reaches of the created universe, however, but on one small planet in that universe. God created both the heavens and the earth but the earth alone is the point of reference. The stars, moon, and sun have a grandeur all their own, but they are made "to give light *on the earth*" (1:5).

As God began to work with the earth it was "formless and void" (1:2), a lump of clay ready to be molded. Then the author of Genesis unfolds the dramatic diversity of the creation. God creates by making a series of differentiations of the "formless and void" earth. Light and darkness are separated; then heaven and earth; then land and sea (1:3-10). God accomplishes all these things by a mere word—his command "Let there be. . . "

Next, God's command brings forth life: plants, fish, birds, land animals, and insects are all called into being (1:11-25). Each new part of creation is different than everything which has come before it, yet all these diverse works of the first five days of creation rush past us. God pauses only briefly to give the benediction "It is good" to each day.

On the sixth day, the speed of creation slows almost to a halt. Now God, who had created everything instantly and without question, turns to a consultation: "Let us make man in our image, after our likeness" (1:26). It's as if God hurried through the creation of the rest of the vast universe, breathed a sigh, and said, "The preliminaries are finished. Let's create the one who will bear our image." Before creating man, the Triune God held a consultation and agreed to proceed. God gave special care to this particular act not because the creation of man required more of his power or wisdom, but because man was to be unique in the entire universe—he was to be the bearer of God's image.

Man, though he was the last created thing, was given dominion over all that had come before him. God's charge to man that he should rule the earth is given twice, first indirectly (1:26) and then directly. He told the man and the woman, "Have dominion over the fish of the sea and over the birds of the air and over every living thing that moves upon the earth" (1:28).

The repetition of this command to rule is not without importance. It emphasizes the uniqueness of man in the created order: He is to govern God's creation as its vice-ruler under God himself. Man's governorship was not to be dictatorial, but was to emulate God's own loving rule, so the man and woman are given the additional charge to take only plants for food (1:29). Man's rule over creation never gave him the right to pervert it for his own selfish ends. He was to rule creation not as a foolish despot, but as a conscientious caretaker.

Genesis 1 says very clearly that man is the climax of God's creation. He is given governorship over God's world because he stands pre-eminent in that world. Man's pre-eminence is summarized in the title he holds as God's image bearer. All the creation witnesses to the nature and power of God (Rom 1:20), but only man bears God's image. He is a "special" creation in the fullest sense of the word, for he is the governor of the world and the image bearer of God.

Man: The Center of Creation

The whole creation story is told once again starting with Genesis 2:6. This kind of repetition is a method the scriptures often use to emphasize something important. The two creation stories tell of the one creation in two different ways. These two different perspectives give us better insight into God's purposes in creating. The Genesis 2 account of creation is the perfect partner of the Genesis 1 account, giving us an added understanding of an event which cannot be properly comprehended from one perspective alone. In fact, Jesus deliberately quotes from both stories in the same sentence (Mt 19:4-5) because, as far as he was concerned, the two together formed one story.

The Genesis 1 account uses the earth as the reference point for all creation. It could be called a "geo-centric" perspective. Genesis 2 further narrows the focus of the story from the earth to man alone on the earth. It moves from a "geo-centric" to an "anthropo-centric" perspective. Man is now the reference point for creation.

The second story restates each aspect of the creation, but this time each event emphasizes the centrality of man. We begin again with a bare earth. There is no vegetation on the ground. The reason is not only that vegetation had not been made yet, but also because "there was no man to till the ground" (2:5). The animals are created as helpers for man (2:18-20), not just for their own sake. As in Genesis 1, the creation of man in Genesis 2 is unique. Here God forms man from the dust and breathes into his nostrils, intimately involving himself with his image bearer (2:7).

The thrust of this repetition of the creation story is that man is the center of God's creation as well as its climax. All other life on earth is to be ordered by him. The plants are not merely to be "kept," but to be "cultivated" (2:15), an activity which calls on man to work creatively with the creation he rules.

In a similar act of creative rule, man names the animals (2:19-20). We will miss the significance of Adam's action if we think of these names merely as unimportant labels; rather, by naming the animals, Adam classified them in his own creative order and identified each uniquely in relationship to himself. That splendid yellow beast over there was no longer a nameless animal — it was "lion." The tall, proud one was now "horse." And the funny-looking one — that one is "goat."

By naming the animals, Adam creatively assigned worth to each one. The narrative explicitly states that "whatever the man called a living creature, that was its name." When man demonstrated his creative rule over the animals by choosing their names, there was no argument from any other created being, nor even from God. It was God's will that man be the focus of the creation and that every part of it should take its identity from him.

The two accounts of the creation, both the geo-centric and the anthropo-centric, make it clear that man was created as a majestic creature, unique in all the earth. He is portrayed as both the climax (first story) and the center (second story) of the creation. He is uniquely created from the dust, uniquely commanded to be God's vice-governor, and uniquely called to be the image bearer of God. The psalmist was right when he said, "Yet thou hast made him little less than God, and dost crown him with glory and honor."

"You Will Be Like God"

Embedded in the second creation story, however, is one element not present in the first. This element is the turning point of all that follows. When he placed man in the garden, God told him,

"You may freely eat of every tree of the garden; but of the tree of knowledge of good and evil you shall not eat, for in the day that you eat of it you shall die" (2:16-17). In the context of Genesis 2, this command doesn't seem to be very important. It is passed over as something which could hardly be otherwise. The possibility of disobedience seems slight — after all, why would a man and a woman living in the Garden of Eden choose to die?

Nonetheless, the implications of this command are far from small. This was not just any tree, but the tree of "knowledge of good and evil." Whoever ate its fruit would obtain a personal, experiential knowledge of good and evil. Because of the nature of this tree, God's prohibition of its fruit was not arbitrary. It gave the man and the woman a choice of ultimate authority. The issue for Adam and Eve was this: Will we rely on God to order our lives, or will we usurp that authority for ourselves and choose the direction for our own lives?

The tree presented Adam and Eve with the choice of living in dependence on God or living independently from him. Knowledge of good and evil would allow them to live egocentrically, without reference to God's authority in matters of good and evil. Soon the serpent brought the choice between a God-centered dependence and a self-centered independence into the foreground.

The choice of ultimate authority forms the crux of the serpent's temptation in Genesis 3. Deliberately opposing God, it says, "You will not die. For God knows that when you eat of it your eyes will be opened, and *you will be like God*, knowing good and evil" (3:4-5). The essence of the serpent's temptation had nothing to do with apples or with hunger. It centers on a desire to "be like God." When Adam and Eve chose to be like God, they chose to take their identities from themselves and recognize no authority except their own. Instead of living as the bearers of his image, reflecting their identity from God, they chose to believe the ephemeral promise of the serpent and to "be like God."

The result of this choice was clearly spelled out in God's original command: death. We will miss the point of this penalty if we think of death as cessation of existence, for the scriptures do not think of it in this way. The Bible sees death not as a cessation but as a separation. Physical death is not the end of man, but is a separation of the inner person from the body. Ultimately, God will bring the two back together for judgment, and in the interim the person who has died physically is in the unnatural state of being separated from his body. But even in this period between death and judgment, the person has by no means ceased to exist.

Similarly, spiritual death is not a cessation of the spiritual dimension of human life, but is rather a separation of man from God. When Adam and Eve chose to disobey God, the penalty was not only one aspect of death, but death in every sphere of their lives. We might even call their penalty "utter death" because their rebellion against God made the tragic separations of death utterly encompass them and touch every part of their existence.

The first result of choosing to "be like God" was that Adam and Eve were separated from each other. Genesis says, "Then the eyes of both were opened, and they knew that they were naked; and they sewed fig leaves together and made themselves aprons" (3:7). Those whom God had made to be "one flesh" were now embarrassed at the sight of each other's flesh. They hid themselves from each other with leaves — a physical sign of their estrangement. There was a separation, a death, in the "one flesh" relationship of Adam and Eve.

Adam and Eve not only hid themselves from each other, but they hid themselves from God. When "they heard the sound of the Lord God walking in the garden in the cool of the day, the man and his wife hid themselves from the presence of the Lord God among the trees of the garden" (3:8). It is difficult for us to imagine the intimacy of their relationship with their Creator before the fall. As God "walked" in the garden, he must surely have "walked" with the man and the woman. But now the tenderness of that relationship was lost, and replaced by fear. Adam and Eve hid from God, acting out the separation they felt from him. There was death in this relationship too.

Eventually, the "utter death" caused by the fall worked itself out in physical death as well. The fall not only separated the man from the woman and from God, but it ultimately separated him from himself. His unity of body and soul dissolved into the separation of death.

The disastrous results of Adam's disobedience were not confined only to the "utter death" of man. His fall brought about the fall of the whole creation. Because man was primary and central in the creation, creation could not stand without him and was subjected to death just as he was. God said to man, "Cursed is the ground *because of you*" (3:17), confirming the separation man's sin had accomplished. The creation which man cultivated in the garden before the fall would now bring forth "thorns and thistles" in rebellion against him. The harmony between man and the rest of the creation was broken—separated. There was death in man's relationship with the earth.

Imagine Adam's horror as he looked around after God's curse. The animals he had named now ran from him! He was ashamed before his wife! And he was afraid of his God! Where there was harmony, there is now separation. Because he is separated from the woman, from the earth, and even from himself, man is no longer "very good." The blessing God pronounced on man and woman at their creation has been violated.

When death entered the human sphere, man was no longer as God had intended him to be. He became, in a real sense, insane—abnormal to the very core of his being. He chose to exalt himself—to be "like God"—rather than to fulfill the function for which God had designed him as his image bearer.

In this cataclysmic fall of man, what was the fate of the image of God? Is man still in some way the majestic image bearer of God, or has he been so badly damaged that nothing at all remains of God's image? We will have to look at other passages of scripture to answer this question.

The Survival of God's Image

The scriptures give us several indications that man in some way still bears God's image even after the fall. In Genesis 9:6, for instance, God sets murder apart as a particularly terrible sin, because man is God's image. "Whoever sheds the blood of man, by man shall his blood be shed; for God made man in his own image." Similarly, James speaks against the evil of cursing men "who are made in the likeness of God" (Jas 3:9).

Both these commands are universal in application and would lose their force if there was nothing left of God's image in man. Man's place as the image bearer of God even forms the basis for an ordinance in the Corinthian church: "A man ought not to cover his head, since he is the image and glory of God" (1 Cor 11:7). We will deal with the argument of this passage in a later chapter. For now all we need to do is notice that it implies that the image of God survived the fall. Paul is speaking specifically *to* Christians in this passage, but he is not speaking only *of* Christians. He is saying something that is true for the whole human race.

These passages all indicate that the image of God was not totally destroyed at the fall. Thus, Adam and Eve, as bearers of God's image, were the parents of an entire race of image bearers. Adam's geneology in the scriptures gives his role as image bearer an interesting twist. "This is the book of the generations of Adam. When God created man, *he made him in the likeness of God....* When Adam had lived a hundred and thirty years, he became the father of a son *in his own likeness, after his image,* and named him Seth" (Gn 5:1,3). Although Adam's creation in God's image is reaffirmed, his children are said to be in *Adam's* image. Thus Adam remained God's image bearer after the fall and transmitted that role to his children. But because the image of God in Adam was damaged by his disobedience, the image he passed down to his children was damaged as well. In any case, the children bore *Adam's* image. Adam's children remain God's image bearers to the extent that Adam himself remained God's image bearer.

Thus the image of God is so deeply imprinted on man's being that it survived the catastrophic consequences of the fall, even though it was severely damaged. In this context, the second commandment is partly a testimony to man's uniqueness as God's image bearer. The commandment says, "You shall not make yourself a graven image, or any likeness of anything that is in heaven above, or that is in the earth beneath, or that is in the water under the earth; you shall not bow down to them or serve them; for I the Lord your God am a jealous God...." (Ex 20:4-5). Golden calves, gods of wood, stone, or metal are dead things. They are the products of man's hands; they cannot be like God in any way. Only man, who is alive and is the product of God's hands, can bear his image.

Just as Adam's son was a living representation of Adam and bore his image, so man is in some way a living representation of God. Of course, man is not God; he is not worthy of worship. Still, he remains somehow the *living* reflection of God himself. The prophets made it clear that the "deadness" of idols was one of the reasons behind the prohibition of idolatry. For example, after one of his denunciations of idols, Jeremiah says, "But the Lord is the true God; he is the *living God* and the everlasting King" (Jer 10:10). To call a dead thing the image of the living God is great blasphemy. Somehow, God designed man so that he alone could be considered his image bearer, a reflection of who God himself is.

In fact, to call man the image bearer of God is the very opposite of idolatry. God is not anthropomorphic — made like man. Rather man is *theo*morphic — made like God. Thus it is nonsense to attempt to make gods in *our* image, for we ourselves bear God's image. But because we are theomorphic, shaped after God's likeness, the scriptures can use anthropomorphic language about God.

In fact, the use of anthropomorphic illustration can provide us with our first glimpse of what it means to be the image bearers of God. Anthropomorphic devices depend on similarities between God and man even though they are not intended to portray literal similarities. When the psalm says that "the eyes of the Lord are toward the righteous" (Ps 34:15), its point is not that God has physical eyes, but that God *sees* his people. He is personally involved with them; he sees them and helps them. This poetic device can be used because God and man are alike in this way — both can see and be personally involved with those around them.

Scripture never uses these anthropomorphic correspondences with reference to the infiniteness of God's divine nature. In fact, God's power, knowledge, and so on are often contrasted to man's limited creaturely nature. Concerning God's truthfulness, for example, scripture says, "God is *not a man*, that he should lie, nor a son of man, that he should repent" (Nm 23:19). As God, he is infinitely and qualitatively different from us. However, both God and man are personal beings. In this sense, we correspond to him.

Virtually every time the Bible uses an anthropomorphic device, it is working with this correspondence between God and man as personal beings. We have already noted one such instance: God "walked in the garden" (Gn 3:8). This does not mean that God got his feet muddy if he stepped in a puddle. Rather, it is a picturesque way of saying that God's relationship to man and his creation was an intimate thing—like that of a man who walks with his friends in a beautiful garden.

The Image of God: Personalness

All of scripture assumes the personalness of both God and man. However, it is almost impossible to define this quality adequately. What does it mean to be a person? Every definition is disputed and beset with problems. This seems odd, for we are more familiar with our own personhood than almost anything else. Fortunately, this familiarity with our personhood allows us to work with personalness intuitively. We know what it is like to be persons, even if we cannot define it precisely. For our purposes, it is easier to work with our intuition of what it means to be a person than it would be to work with an abstract definition.

However we describe this quality of personalness which we all possess, it is in our personhood that we correspond to God. He is not an impersonal All as in Buddhism, nor is he just the First Cause as in Deism. He is personal—in the same way that we are personal. In our common existence as personal beings we are like God, and as personal beings we bear his image.

Our personalness is also the point where we differ from the rest of the creation. I am like God because we are both personal beings. I am different from a tree because I am a personal being and it is not. In all the creation, only man is personal in this sense. Dogs, monkeys, and computers, although they mimic personal behavior or display some characteristics which we associate with the personal, do not possess the kind of personhood we do. The similarities between man and the rest of the creation are great, but so are the differences, These differences can be summed up in this category of personalness.

God expected man to rule the earth personally, as his vice-governor. Man was not to rule despotically over the creation, but to co-labor creatively with the creation. We have seen the creativity which God expected of his image bearer when he called him to cultivate the garden and to name the animals. This was the flavor of Adam and Eve's rule of the creation: joyful co-laboring, not fear and struggle. Man's dominion in the creation was to be marked by great beauty. He would leave the unique marks of his personality on the world around him. No one could have cultivated the garden into quite the same patterns as Adam did, for he would leave the mark of his unique personality as God's image bearer on the garden. By changing the order of the creation, man brought himself personally, as the image bearer of God, into relationship with the rest of the creation.

Man's creation as a personal being leaves an important question: Does man's personhood *exhaust* the meaning of his creation in the image of God? All of the tasks God gave him — ruling the earth, cultivating the garden, naming the animals — reflect this unique personhood. But is this all? Is there more involved in bearing the image of God?

The Whole Person as God's Image

In the biblical view, our nature as personal beings certainly does not exhaust the meaning of our role as God's image bearers. If it did, we would be confronted with all sorts of problems. For instance, man's ability to reason surely forms a part of his personalness. But, as Martin Luther said, if that's what it means to be an image bearer of God, then Satan is a better image bearer than we are, for he is certainly more intelligent than a mere human being! Or consider the ability to make moral choices, another important aspect of our personhood. Yet this ability is exactly the place where the serpent tempted Adam and Eve and where they fell. He promised that they would "be like God" if they could distinguish good and evil without reference to God. However, this ability took them further from God.

The scriptural understanding of the image of God is more than the mere fact of personhood. Man's personhood is only the *basis* of his image bearing, not the reality itself. This richness of man's role as God's image surfaces in a number of places. Consider the account of man's creation. Genesis makes only one comment on man's role as bearer of God's image: "And God created man in his own image, in the image of God he created him; *male and female he created them*" (1:27). We tend to read right over this comment, thinking, "Of course, how else could he have made us?" Although God created some of the other creatures as male and female, Genesis doesn't think that this is important enough to record. The other animals are simply told to "be fruitful and multiply."

The remark that God created man in his image as specifically "male and female" should stop us. We should be shocked at what the text says! Surely such an unexpected comment is of great significance, especially since it is the only statement we have in context about the meaning of man's image bearing. Many of the animals were created male and female. Why does scripture emphasize the fact that we are male and female in the account of the creation of God's image bearer?

One problem with this comment is that our sexuality is one way in which we obviously *don't* resemble God. Is God somehow half male and half female? Of course not. How then does being male and female have anything to do with being bearers of God's image? This problem should show us that personalness does not exhaust the concept of the image of God.

Another clue that personalness in itself is an incomplete description of image bearing is the connection between the resurrection of the body and the image of God. In 1 Corinthians 15, Paul caps his argument for the existence of a resurrection body with the statement, "Just as we have borne the image of the man of dust [Adam], we shall also bear the image of the man of heaven [Christ]" (1Cor 15:49). Paul is saying that *in* our new bodies we will become image bearers of God in a more complete sense. God's plan for us is not just to save our souls. If that were the case, why should he bother resurrecting our bodies?

Apparently, God's goal is not just saving souls, but saving his image bearers. Since our salvation ultimately involves our bodies as well as our personalities, could it be that somehow our bodies are involved in bearing God's image? Although such an idea seems foolish to us, it did not seem foolish to the biblical authors. We have inherited a Greek understanding of man which splits him into two parts: an immortal soul living inside a mortal body. This view of man is foreign to the authors of the Old and New Testaments.

The Bible views man as a unity. He is a soulish-body or a bodily-soul but not a body//soul. The inner man and the outer man are not sharply separated in the scriptures, even though we tend to read that division into them. Instead, body and soul are two interrelated aspects of the one being — man.

The apostles use this unified concept of man when they talk about his role as the image bearer of God. Thus we should not be shocked when they imply that God's image encompasses us as whole beings, bodies included. For example, John says that when Christ appears "we shall be like him" (1 Jn 3:2). That is, we shall bear his image in a more complete way. Is it just coincidental that this will happen at the time when we receive our new bodies?

To this we could add 2 Corinthians 5:1-8 where Paul views being "naked" (meaning existence as a disembodied personality) with great distaste. He longs to be clothed with his "heavenly dwelling" (his resurrection body), but he comforts himself that he will at least be "at home with the Lord" even if he doesn't get his new body right away.

In these and other places, the biblical view of man as a unified being comes through clearly. We seldom think in these terms, for we have long been steeped in thought patterns which divide man into body and soul (usually exalting the soul as good and making the body its enemy). But we need to remember that we have Plato and not Paul to thank for these thought patterns. Paul and John and the rest of the apostles had no problem seeing the body as part of the image of God, because man was a unity and if he bore God's image it extended to his whole being — body included.

The concept of man as a unified being underlies every part of the biblical discussion of his nature. For example, the apostles invariably judge matters of sexual ethics from the perspective of man's unity. Many people today describe the homosexual as someone with the soul of one sex trapped inside the body of the other sex. They demand that the soul be allowed sexual expression in contradiction to the sex of the body. This notion is intolerable to the biblical view of man because it divides the body and the soul. How dare we deny the unity of man so completely that the soul is opposed to the body? How can we affirm the soul's sexual orientation by denying the body's sexual orientation? The apostles always viewed homosexuality as an aberration which betrays the tragic fallenness of man and the separations resulting from sin.

To return to our point, the biblical implication that the body also bears the image of God means that we cannot view that image only in terms of personalness. If being image bearers just means that we are personal beings and nothing more, there would be no need for our bodies to be resurrected on the last day. We could exist eternally as disembodied "personalities" and still fulfill our role as God's image bearers.

Thus we cannot view our role as bearers of God's image only in terms of personalness. This view does not account for some aspects of what it means to be a person. It does not help us understand the creation of man as male and female. It cannot deal with the biblical concept of the body as part of the image of God. Indeed personalness is not all there is to the image of God. In the scriptures, the idea of image bearing is both broader and more profound. Personalness forms the framework of understanding what it means to bear the image of God, but the content of that image is in personal relationships—namely, man's relationship with God and man's relationship with man. Only in these relationships does man's true nature as God's image bearer come to light.

The Image of God: Relationships

Scripture nowhere gives us a systematized description of man. No book of the Bible is called "The Christian View of Man." Instead, the Bible teaches us who we are as human beings by describing and reflecting on the way God works in history. The author of Genesis deals with who man is by using this historical method of teaching. He deliberately includes several subsequent events in the section describing man's creation and fall. This inclusion is accomplished by using the literary device "these are the generations of" (2:4; 5:1; 6:9; 10:1; 11:10; 11:27; 25:12; 36:1; 36:9; 37:2), usually followed by a geneology. This divides the monumental amount of material contained in the book of Genesis into several convenient and unified sections.

Genesis 1:1-2:4, the first of these unified sections, deals with the creation with the earth as its reference point. Genesis 2:5-5:1, the next section, uses man as the reference point. This anthropocentric section, from the beginning of the "second" creation story (2:5) and ending in Adam's geneology (5:1), is one unified whole introduced and concluded by the device "these are the generations of." By using this device, Genesis intimately links man's creation and fall to two other events: the expulsion from the Garden and Cain's murder of Abel.

Thus if Genesis deliberately links the expulsion of Adam and Eve from the Garden (3:22-24) and the story of Cain and Abel (4:1-24) to man's creation and fall, it seems reasonable to consider these events in light of man's place in the creation. By putting them in the immediate context of the fall, the writer meant to teach us that these were direct results of the fall; this expulsion and this murder are not merely unrelated events that happened some time after man's creation and corruption. Indeed, this section closes with the words, "When God created man, he made him in the likeness of God" (5:1). This is the overall theme of this section of Genesis — the nature and fate of God's image bearer. Thus the fate of Adam and Eve and the story of Cain and Abel reveal something of what the image of God is by describing the dramatic changes which occurred in man after the fall.

The first of these related events, the expulsion of Adam and Eve from the garden, follows the curse God placed upon them. The reason why the Lord dismissed them from his presence was lest they "put forth their hand and take also of the tree of life, and eat, and live for ever" (Gn 3:22). The stated penalty for their act of rebellion was "in the day that you eat of it [the tree] you shall die" (Gn 2:17). They did not die physically on that day, but the separations of "utter death" began immediately with the sundering of their relationships with God and with each other. The expulsion of Adam and Eve from the garden sealed that death by forcing them to depart from God's presence, making their separation from him a physical reality. Thus the fall broke the relationship between man and God. This was "spiritual death;" man was separated from him who is the only source of life.

The account of Cain and Abel tells about the analogous separation on a human level—what we could call "social death." The rivalry between Cain and Abel eventually led to the unprecedented act of murder, a vivid example of the deformed character of human relationships after the fall. Just as Adam and Eve were expelled from the garden, so Cain was "driven from the ground" (4:14) and "dwelt in the land of wandering" (4:16) as a result of his sin.

Just as the expulsion of Adam and Eve from the Garden made concrete their loss of an intimate relationship with God, so the expulsion of Cain from the ground made concrete his loss of intimate relationship with other men. Cain's punishment meant that he would no longer have social "roots." He would have to dwell in the "land of wandering" (the literal meaning of "Nod") all his life. His nomadic existence was to epitomize the broken character of human relationships after the fall.

From these two events, we can infer some things about the status of the image of God before the fall. Initially, the bearers of God's image possessed two unique relationships: the personal relationship between man and God and the personal relationship between man and man (Adam and Eve). These two types of intimate relationships were the content of the image of God before the fall. The personalness of man is the foundation of the image of God, for it makes him capable of relationships. But the building itself is this pair of personal relationships toward God and toward man.

The author of Genesis takes pains to point out that the entrance of death into these two relationships is the key to the effects of the fall. These effects did not primarily apply to man as a living being (although physical death did enter his world) or to man as the creative governor of the earth (although this was affected as well), or to man's nature as a personal, thinking creature. The fall primarily affected man in his role as the bearer of God's image—that is, man in relationship to God and to man. Man bore God's image as he functioned in these two personal relationships. And when God's image bearer fell, he disrupted these two personal relationships.

However, this disruption did not totally destroy either man's relationship with God or his relationship with man. Eve praised God at Cain's birth (4:1); Cain and Abel offered sacrifices to him (4:3-4); and Cain was in "the presence of the Lord" (4:16) when he received his sentence. A relationship between man and God still exists, but we no longer see the intimate encounter with God "walking in the Garden." Instead, the relationship is often characterized by fear instead of joyous intimacy. We could almost say that man's relationship with God was *negativized* by the fall, for man's love toward God has changed into its negative—fear.

Man's relationship with man suffered in an analogous way. Adam and Eve still lived as husband and wife after the fall; Cain took a wife; and Cain and Abel certainly played together as children. But Cain's smug answer to the Lord's question about Abel, "Am I my brother's keeper?" (4:9) betrayed an attitude of indifference toward his brother rather than a spirit of intimacy with him.

After the fall, human relationships suffered the same mutilation as man's relationship with God; they did not cease to exist, but became qualitatively different. They were not just less intense; they became self-centered and negative. Man had chosen to order his own life and to take his direction from himself. Thus he had turned inward, away from God and other men. As a result, the image of God was deformed.

The most appropriate answer to the question "does fallen man bear the image of God?" is yes, he does, but in a negativized form. His relationships with God and with man were not destroyed at the fall, but rather they were *negativized*. Adam's intimate relationship with God was changed into its negative, into a relationship of rebellion and fear. The mutual love between Cain and Abel was changed into its negative as well, into a self-seeking lust for power and ultimately into murder.

Relationships and the Whole Person

This understanding of the effect of the fall on man opens a new perspective on Jesus' attitude toward the Law. One function of the Law is to show us what it means to be truly human; it is in part a detailed account of what God says man should be like. Thus Jesus revealed something very important about the Law when he summarized it in the two greatest commandments: "You shall love the Lord your God with all your heart, and with all your soul, and with all your mind. This is the great and first commandment. And a second is like it, You shall love your neighbor as yourself. *On these two commandments depend all the law and the prophets*" (Mt 22:37-40). He tells us that to love God (restore the lost vertical relationship) is the basis of everything God intended in the Law. The rest of the Law is an elaboration of these two commands. The Law tells us what the repaired image of God should look like, and it summarizes that repaired image in terms of loving relationships with God and men.

However, this does not account for the implication of the New Testament writers that the body too is the image of God. Why is the body resurrected? Couldn't we have personal relationships (in the sense that we had them before the fall) as disembodied personalities?

The only answer to this question is that we could have relationships without bodies, but that this is not what God wants. He wants us to love him as whole persons. The psalm says, "O God, thou art my God, I seek thee, my *soul* thirsts for thee; my *flesh* faints for thee" (63:1). God's desire for us is that our relationship with him be of the *whole* man; not a "soul love" only, but a "flesh love" as well. Our love for God is to be of the whole person, a yearning of soul *and* body for its Creator.

Paul teaches the same thing, "Present *your bodies* [not just "your souls"] as a living sacrifice, holy and acceptable to God, which is your spiritual worship" (Rom 12:1). We are invited into relationship with God as whole people, including our bodies, even in worship. When the Jews were called to worship the Lord in the synagogue, the *shema* was read, exhorting them, "You shall love the Lord your God with all your heart and with all your soul *and with all your might"* (Dt 6:5). What does this mean except that we are to worship God with our whole beings, including our "might," our physical strength?

This is a likely meaning because the biblical view of man does not resemble our partitioned modern understanding. It always sees man as a whole being, though from different perspectives. The words heart, soul, and might in the *shèma* do not designate three separate parts of man, but are examples of the way the whole man is called to worship. The *shema* commands us to worship God with our entire being—because the entire being is the image of God.

A similar affirmation is involved when Paul tells Timothy, "I desire then that in every place the men should pray, *lifting holy hands"* (1 Tm 2:8). This does not mean that there is something magical about raising your hands when you pray. Rather, Paul wants the whole man—body as well as soul—to be extended toward God in prayer. It seems odd to us that Paul should care about our posture, but on reflection this is not an unusual concern if we are to be in personal relationship with God as whole people. Our bodies and souls are to be directed to God in loving worship.

Our relationships with other men are to be carried out in the same way—by the whole person. John says, "Let us not love in word or speech [that is, not as an internal exercise of the soul], but in deed [in the external physical world] and in truth" (1 Jn 3:18). Of marriage, the closest of all human relationships, Paul says, "Husbands should love their wives *as their own bodies"* (Eph 5:28). Note that Paul did not say "as their own souls" but "as their own *bodies"!*

Marriage is certainly the most intimate example of our relationships with other people, but this idea of loving as whole beings carries over into all human interactions. The command "You shall love your neighbor as yourself" does not just involve "spiritual" love which is never expressed in concrete, mundane acts of caring. If we loved ourselves in that way, we would be in bad shape. All of us care for ourselves as whole persons in many practical ways. We eat, sleep, exercise, study, and so on. This is the kind of practical love for the whole person that we are called to show to others.

The implication of this is that the image of God could not be borne by a disembodied spirit, but only by a whole human being. This seems to be the reasoning Paul and the other apostles used to deduce the resurrection of the body from the fact that man bears God's image.

The concept that the image of God involves the Godward and manward relationships also contains the key for understanding Genesis' comment that man was created in God's image as "male and female." The animals were created in male/female pairs for the purpose of reproduction. God's purpose for creating man as male and female included this, but is also enabled his image bearer to be in truly personal manward relationships. If man had only been created as a single unit and not as a pair (male and female), there would have been no possibility of bearing the horizontal facet of the image of God. This does not mean, of course, that the only true horizontal relationship is between a man and a woman. Genesis uses the creation of man as male and female as a metaphor for all human personal relationships. Not only the man-woman relationship but all human relationships are affirmed as part of the creation of mankind in the image of God. When God created man in his image, he created them male and female so they could enter into personal relationships with each other as well as with him. Because they were in these horizontal and vertical relationships, men could truly bear God's image.

The creation of man in the image of God is one of the foundation stones in the biblical basis of Christian community. The loving horizontal and vertical relationships which characterize the image of God are the very things which are to be reflected in Christian community. At this point, we can say that Christian community is scriptural, at least with respect to man's creation in the image of God. Its two-fold structure fits very well with the two-fold structure of God's image in loving relationships with others and with God.

The Unresolved Tension

These horizontal and vertical relationships which make up the image of God still exist after the fall, but they were grievously damaged in that disaster. Man still bears God's image, but in a corrupted, deformed, and negativized way. We are left with relationships which are negativized: self-centered and full of fear. They are only memories of the glorious things which once were.

The continued existence of the image of God in men does not give men any reason to boast before God. He is no less fallen or less sinful than he would be if the image of God had been totally erased by the fall. The continuance of the image gives him no special standing. It means only that man lives in a constant tension and contradiction, caught between who he should be as the image bearer of God and who he is as a fallen creature.

Thus we should not be surprised that man's behavior is full of inconsistencies: rationality and irrationality, bravery and cowardice, the demonic and the divine. These inconsistencies flow from a great rift in man's character. He finds himself in a struggle between the wonder of his creation and the horror of his fall. However, God's desire for man is not to leave him forever caught in this tension, but to bring him back from the devastation of the fall. The resolution of the tension between creation and fall belongs to a third event in man's history—the new creation in Jesus Christ.

TWO

REDEMPTION AND COMMUNITY: THE RENEWED IMAGE

T HE fall is the root of mankind's great identity crisis. Because we are alienated from our Creator, we have no suitable source from which to take our identity. Had we not fallen, we could naturally take up our proper place as creatures before God and understand ourselves in relation to him. However, we are separated from him who should be our reference point.

In our fallen state, we try to take our identity from things in the creation rather than from God the Creator. These solutions to our common identity crisis are good examples of the tragedy of our fallenness. We take things which are not bad in themselves, and turn them into evil because we try to make *them* the root of our lives. We make good parts of the creation into false gods. Many people's lives are consumed by the pursuit of possessions, for example. Making extra bucks to buy that new car becomes their reason for living, and such people end up taking their identity from the things in their lives. Possessions in themselves are not bad of course, but when they become the center of our lives, the source of our identity, we fall under the condemnation of the rich young man in Mark 10:17-31.

I know a woman who made her children the center of her life. She spared herself no pain in raising them. She constantly sacrificed for them, and did everything for their benefit. But as her children grew older, they felt smothered by her self-sacrifice. One by one they moved away from home and the mother was left alone. She spent several years in a state of severe depression which only gradually diminished. Why? Because in her zeal to be a good mother, she had taken her identity from her children. When they were gone, there was nothing left of her. There is nothing wrong with loving one's children. But as fallen people, we seem particularly perverse in our ability to turn good things into evil by taking our ultimate identity from them, rather than from God. This ability to turn good into evil should constantly remind us that we are terribly damaged in our relationships and are in dire need of renewal.

Any parent can testify to the dilemmas encountered in trying to raise children. When should you be flexible? When should you be firm? When does mother love turn into "smother love?" These dilemmas point up our basic human condition: We are caught between the beauty of our creation and the horror of our fall. The fact that we can even talk about love is a reminder that we are the glorious image bearers of God. But even love has a two-edged character which, paradoxical as it seems, can be used for either good or evil. This is part of the tragedy of fallen man. Even our best characteristics have been disfigured by our fall.

A New Creation

The Bible, while brutally realistic about man's basic dilemmas, provides true hope that our state of fallenness is not permanent. According to scripture, the conflict between man's created glory and fallen depravity has already been resolved in principle. God has made a radical reformulation of man himself — a reformulation so complete it can only be called a "new creation." Paul says, "If any one is in Christ, he is a new creation; the old has passed away, behold, the new has come" (2 Cor 5:17). The new creation is already present in the old, but is still awaiting its total fulfillment. This new creation is not just an amended version of man. It is the first step of a process that will eventually result in the renewal of the whole created order.

The new creation is a third cataclysmic event in man's history, one that has affected him as radically as his creation and fall.

Something utterly new in history took place when "the Word became flesh and dwelt among us" (Jn 1:14). The coming of Jesus Christ was the event that had been prophesied for centuries. It was the redemption which God's people had been awaiting since Adam's time. The coming of Jesus had been woven into the fabric of God's dealings with man ever since the fall, but when he came, something new happened. In Christ, the new creation was begun.

The gospel writers portray Jesus as the beginning of something new in human history, something as crucial to man as his creation and fall. To emphasize this newness in Christ, both Matthew and John allude to Genesis at the opening of their gospels. Matthew begins with a geneology, choosing a form reminiscent of the "these are the generations of" device that is used over and over in Genesis. He traces Jesus' kingly descent all the way back to Abraham, thus implying a parallel between the events of Genesis and the events of his gospel.

John draws an even more explicit parallel. He directs his readers right to Genesis 1:1 by using language reminiscent of the opening words of the creation story. Genesis starts "In the beginning God created the heavens and the earth." John says "In the beginning was the Word." The parallel is striking, and intentional. Genesis told of the creation, but John tells of the *new* creation.

The Second Adam

The idea of Christ's work as a new creation is found not only in the gospels but also explicitly in the letters of Paul. Paul leaves us in no doubt that the work of Christ is a third important event in man's history, along with the creation and the fall, for he speaks of Christ as a "second Adam." Paul deals with the concept of Jesus as a second Adam in two long passages — Romans 5:12-19 and 1 Corinthians 15:21-24 — both of which we will examine presently. Although the scripture's teaching on the subject is drawn out most fully in these places, they are not the only statements on the subject. Rather they are part of the atmosphere which underlies the entire biblical understanding of Christ's mission.

The parallel between Adam and Christ, the second Adam, surfaces continually in the New Testament. Luke, for example, recognized the parallel between Adam's temptation in Eden and
Jesus' temptation in the wilderness. His geneology of Jesus does
not stop with Abraham, but continues back to Adam, whom he
calls "the son of God" (Lk 3:38). Two sentences later, Luke
records Satan's temptation of Jesus beginning with the words, "If
you are the Son of God..." (Lk 4:3). It is no accident that Luke
calls both Adam and Jesus "the son of God" in such close proximi-
ty. He clearly intended to imply that Adam ("the son of God")
and Jesus ("the Son of God") are parallel figures in human history. Adam failed when he was tempted in the garden; Jesus tri-
umphed when he was tempted in the wilderness. The two Adams
stand in parallel: One is the source of defeat, the other is the
source of victory.

Another example of the parallel between Adam and Christ is
found in the references to Jesus as "the image of God" (2 Cor 4:4;
Heb 1:3). To call Jesus "the image of God" does not deny his
equality as God with the Father and the Holy Spirit. However,
when we affirm the deity of Christ, we must be careful not to lose
sight of his complete humanity. Paul had no qualms about saying
"there is one mediator between God and men, *the man* Christ
Jesus" (1 Tm 2:5), and we are in serious difficulty if we cannot say
it as well. If we deny the manhood of our savior, we deny his
identification with us and deny the value of his work. The meaning of his work is affirmed precisely in the fact that the man
Christ Jesus is the image of God. He stands in a unique place, parallel to the first Adam, and man with us.

Paul draws out the position of Jesus as a second Adam in detail.
In Romans 5, as an argument for the certainty of our salvation, he
places Adam and Christ side by side and shows that the ministry
of the second Adam, Christ, is utterly superior to that of the first:

Therefore, just as sin entered the world through one man, and
death through sin, and in this way death came to all men, because all sinned — for before the law was given, sin was in the
world. But sin is not taken into account when there is no law.
Nevertheless, death reigned from the time of Adam to the time

of Moses, even over those who did not sin by breaking a command, as did Adam, who was a pattern of the one to come.

But the gift is not like the trespass. For if many died by the trespass of the one man, how much more did God's grace and the gift that came by the grace of the one man, Jesus Christ, overflow to the many! Again, the gift of God is not like the result of the one man's sin: The judgment followed one sin and brought condemnation, but the gift followed many trespasses and brought justification. For if, by the trespass of the one man, death reigned through that one man, how much more will those who receive God's abundant provision of grace and of the gift of righteousness reign in life through the one man, Jesus Christ.

Consequently, just as the result of one trespass was condemnation for all men, so also the result of one act of righteousness was justification that brings life for all men. For just as through the disobedience of the one man the many were made sinners, so also through the obedience of the one man the many will be made righteous. (Rom 5:12-19)

To understand Paul's argument, we must first understand the concept of federal headship — the idea that makes the argument work. Paul sees Adam and Christ as something like the chiefs of two different tribes or clans. Whatever the chief decides, the whole clan does — the tribe stands in solidarity behind its chief. The tribe does not precisely *choose* to follow its chief (although it does). There are simply no other options. He is the chief; the clan follows him. The idea of a chief as a "federal head" of his people is unfamiliar to us, but this was a feature of human society for many centuries. This is how missionaries made many converts in the Middle Ages. If they could convert the chief of a tribe to Christianity, they would baptize the whole tribe. The members of the tribe stood in solidarity with their chief. They did not have to decide individually to become Christians; the chief's choice *was* their choice. Of course they would follow him; after all, he was the head.

The solidarity of a clan under its chief is foreign to us, but it was a basic part of the thinking of ancient Israel. The Old Testament is full of examples of this kind of solidarity under a federal head. For instance, because the sons of Levi stood with Moses (and with the Lord) during the golden calf incident, their tribe was made the priestly tribe (Ex 32:19-29). The loyalty of the sons of Levi had a permanent result for their descendants. Whether their children were faithful or not, they reaped the benefits of their fathers' actions. The fathers had acted as federal heads for their children.

The argument of Romans 5 is based on this same concept of federal headship. Because Adam was head over all humanity as the chief of our clan, we are all implicated in what he did. His choice to live in independence from God *was* our choice as well. When he sinned, we sinned, because Adam was our head. This is why Paul says "many died [reaped the penalty of sin] by the trespass of the one man [*not* by many trespasses]" (Rom 5:15).

Thus, employing this idea of federal headship, Paul divides all humanity into two clans: those under Adam and those under Christ. His intent is to show the utter superiority of Christ's ministry as head of redeemed humanity. However, in verse 14, he speaks of Adam as "a *pattern* of the one to come," namely, Christ. Though his argument contrasts Jesus and Adam, it is based on certain striking similarities between them.

1. *Adam and Christ are both chiefs of their clans.*

Adam and Christ are both federal heads. Adam was chief of the clan of humanity and our relationship to him must be understood in terms of his decisive actions. In a similar way, Jesus Christ is the head of the clan of redeemed humanity. Adam's actions resulted in death for us; Christ's actions resulted in life. Each acted as head of a clan — one to make us sinners, the other to make us righteous (Rom 5:19).

2. *Adam and Christ are both unique bearers of God's image.*

Both Adam and Christ are prototype image bearers of God. By God's special creation, Adam was made from the dust of the earth. Before the fall, he was perfectly "the image and glory of God" (1 Cor 11:7). The creation of an image bearer was God's unique act, and Adam stands as a prototype for all men — bearers of God's image even after the fall (Gn 5:1-3).

Jesus is also the prototype image bearer of God, yet in a far superior way. Adam was "the image and glory of God," but Jesus is "the radiance of God's glory and the *exact representation* of his being" (Heb 1:3). When Adam was created, the universe saw God's image and glory. When "the Word became flesh," it saw not only God's image, but the "*exact representation* of his being;" it saw not only his glory, but the "*radiance*" of his glory. Christ could be called "the ultimate Adam" — what Adam was in type, Christ was in fullness. Like Adam, Christ was also to be head of a new race of image bearers.

3. *Adam and Christ are both "firstborn."*

Another parallel between Jesus and Adam is that both functioned as "firstborn." The firstborn son in ancient societies received a birthright which placed him in a pre-eminent position among the children of the family. He was heir to his father's name and possessions. Scripture sees the concept of firstborn in this same way, but occasionally it separates the idea of pre-eminence from that of priority of birth. David, for instance, was the youngest of Jesse's eight sons, but was nevertheless called "firstborn" because of his pre-eminence as king (Ps 89:27). On the other hand, Reuben had priority among Jacob's sons by birth, but lost his pre-eminence as firstborn (1 Chr 5:1). Joseph's sons became "firstborn" in Reuben's place even though they were born a full generation later. It was they who were given the pre-eminent position.

Christ and Adam can be considered "firstborn" in this sense of pre-eminence of authority and position. Jesus is called "firstborn" in two places (Col 1:15 and Heb 1:6). Although the term is never explicitly applied to Adam, the description fits him quite well. Adam was given pre-eminence over the creation. By virtue of God's command he functioned as firstborn, even though he was the "last born" thing in the creation.

Of course Adam held his position by virtue of the command of God, while Christ has his position by virtue of his nature as God. Paul says "he is the image of the invisible God, the first-born of all creation" (Col 1:15). Calling Christ "firstborn" doesn't mean that he was the first created thing any more than it meant that with reference to Adam. Jesus is "firstborn" because, by his nature as

God, he has pre-eminent authority over all the creation (Col 1:16-17).

Therefore, the first and second Adams are alike in several ways: Each is the head of a clan of mankind; each is a prototypical image bearer of God; and each is pre-eminent as firstborn. Paul's argument in Romans 5 depends on these similarities. But in all these things, Adam "was a pattern of the one to come" (v. 14), implying that in every respect Christ is far superior to Adam. Whereas Adam was "the image of God," Jesus is the "exact representation." Whereas Adam functioned as firstborn by God's command, Christ is firstborn by his very nature as God.

Christ and Adam

Paul's argument in Romans 5 is based both on these similarities between Adam and Christ and the utter superiority of Christ to Adam. Paul then argues by contrasting the headship of Christ to the headship of Adam. Sin entered the world through Adam and brought with it its sure penalty—death (v. 12). Adam sinned by violating an expressed command of God. Because Adam was universal head over humanity, people still died because they had all sinned in Adam (v. 14), even though they did not violate the Law (v. 13). Thus death became universal at the historical moment that Adam sinned. Each of us, though unborn, was a part of his clan; therefore each of us sinned in him (v. 12). His choice *was* our choice. The universality of death is the result of the devastation brought by the fall, and the evidence of our incrimination in Adam's sin.

Paul is saying, "Look, death comes to all men. No exceptions. Death is the penalty for rebellion against God. Everybody dies, even people who don't deliberately rebel against God's Law. How can that be? It happens because Adam acted as our chief when he rebelled against God; his rebellion *was* our rebellion, so we are subject to the penalty of death as well."

Paul continues. The first Adam's sin brought death to all, but the gift of God in the second Adam brought the opposite—life. Adam gave us death, judgment, and condemnation; Christ gave us justification and righteousness. Verse 17 is the climax of his argument: "For if by the trespass of the one man, death reigned through that one man, *how much more* will those who receive God's abundant provision of grace and of the gift of righteousness reign in life through the one man, Jesus Christ." Death is inescapable. But if Adam's headship brought death inescapably, the life that Christ brings is "much more" inescapable because he is far superior to Adam. Christ's gift of life is *even more sure* than death for those who "receive God's abundant provision of grace."

Christ's headship over men and his gift of life revolve around "the obedience of the one man" Christ (v. 19) which Paul contrasts to the disobedience of Adam. Since disobedience brought death, it is understandable that it would take obedience to bring life, but what was Jesus' obedience? We can see this best by recalling the nature of Adam's disobedience.

Adam's sin was essentially rebellion, the desire for self-sufficiency. When the serpent promised Adam and Eve that they would "be like God" if they would disobey his command, they chose to center their lives around themselves instead of around God. Christ's obedience was precisely the opposite of this. Christ, "though he was in the form of God, did not count equality with God a thing to be grasped, but emptied himself" (Phil 2:6-7). Adam, who was not God by nature, desired to be like God. Jesus, who was God by nature, did not proudly hold onto his prerogatives as God, but submitted himself to become a man.

The gospels make this same point many times. They see Christ's whole life as one of obedience to the Father. Over and over Jesus makes statements like, "For I have not spoken on my own authority; the Father who sent me has himself given me commandment what to say and what to speak" (Jn 12:49). Christ's actions are consistently described as being led by the Spirit (see Mt 4:1). The evangelists emphasize Jesus' submissive attitude for very good reason: Since Adam rebelled against God, Jesus had to submit to him if he was to save us. In his submission, Jesus stood as the opposite of Adam. The first Adam desired self-sufficiency; the second Adam submitted to God.

At this point, Paul's concept of the two Adams joins his argument in Romans as a whole. The two Adams are the chiefs of two clans of humanity. One of these clans, Christ's, is based on his obedience. The other, Adam's, is based on his disobedience. The question then is: How does one transfer from Adam's clan to Christ's? The answer, which Paul has been preaching in Romans all along, is "by faith."

The result of Christ's ministry is that "the righteousness of God has been manifested apart from law, although the law and prophets bear witness to it, the righteousness of God through faith in Jesus Christ for all who believe" (Rom 3:21-22). God has manifested his righteousness in Christ and we are sharers in that righteousness by faith.

This is precisely where Paul ends his argument in Romans 5: Christ's "one act of righteousness" (v. 18) is the thing which will make us righteous (v. 19). By faith we change clans, being taken from under Adam's headship and put under Christ's headship. The tremendous result of this change is that we are made righteous. Just as Adam's sin became our sin, so we receive Christ's righteousness as our own.

When we change clans by faith, there is a fundamental change in our relationship with God. Now we are reconciled; we receive a renewed relationship with him (Rom 5:10-11). We are no longer "in Adam" but "in Christ"—that is, we are under his headship.

The sacramental language of baptism says the same thing. Paul asks, "Do you not know that all of us who have been baptized *into Christ Jesus* were baptized into his death? We were buried therefore with him by baptism into death, so that as Christ was raised from the dead by the glory of the Father, *we too might walk in newness of life*" (Rom 6:3-4). In baptism we are called to live out the new life which has already been given to us in Christ.

The key to the new creation in Christ is this righteousness we already have by faith and are called to live out in space and time. The new creation is accomplished in principle and is to be worked out in our lives until Christ returns. Only at that time will it be utterly completed. Paul tells the church at Ephesus to "*put on* [an action in the present] the new man which in likeness of God *has been created* [an action in the past] in righteousness and holiness of the truth" (Eph 4:24). We are already new people by faith, new creations. Paul's exhortation is to "put on" what already "has been created." One might describe our status as "accomplished-but-not-yet-fulfilled" new creations. We have been made renewed image bearers of God. This is an accomplished fact, but its fulfillment is left for the future.

A Renewed Relationship with God

Our new, proper relationship with God is a very specific one. To use John's language, in changing clans, we are "born again" (Jn 3:7) as God's children. "But to all who received him, who believed in his name, he gave power to become children of God; who were born, not of blood nor of the will of the flesh nor of the will of man, but of God" (Jn 1:12-13). Our rebirth as God's children is the renewal of the image of God.

We have noticed that Luke calls both Adam and Christ "son of God" (Lk 3:38; 4:3). Now all of us who come under Christ's headship are referred to as "sons of God" (Gal 3:26; Rom 8:16, etc.). We stand beside Jesus, God's unique only-begotten Son, because we are all God's children by rebirth. Under the headship of the Son of God, our relationship with God becomes one of intimate sonship. This is why the scripture says that Jesus "is not ashamed to call [us] brethren" (Heb 2:11). As re-created image bearers of God, he has brought us to a right relationship with him — a relationship of sonship.

All who come under Christ's headship by faith receive a renewed relationship with God. This is expressed clearly in Galatians 3:26, 28: "For in Christ Jesus you are all sons of God through faith. . . . There is neither Jew nor Greek, there is neither slave nor free, there is neither male nor female." Racial, social, and sexual discriminations are all passed over — all are made children of God equally and without distinction. The Holy Spirit speaks this truth in each of our hearts so we can all cry "Abba, Father" (Gal 4:6), a shout of sheer joy at the intimacy of our relationship with God. We can even dare to call God "Abba" — beloved father, daddy.

John expressed the awesome joy of being in a Father-child relationship with God by saying, "See what love the Father has given us, that we should be called children of God; *and so we are*" (1 Jn 3:1). He follows this with a statement that helps us understand our renewal to the image of God: "Beloved, we are God's children *now*; it does not yet appear *what we shall be*, but we know that

This verse expresses our status as a new creation—"accomplished-but-not-yet-fulfilled." We *are* the children of God, but the time is yet to come when we *will be* sons. What is even more striking is the link between sonship and bearing God's image. John says that when "we will be" sons, "we shall be like him." Scripture makes the same connection in noting Seth's birth in Genesis 5:3. Adam "became the father of a son in his own likeness, after his image, and named him Seth." As Adam's son, Seth bore his image. As children of God, we "will be like him"—that is, we will bear his image. Being sons of God is at the core of bearing the image of God, for sonship is the relationship which the bearers of God's image have with him.

Paul brings out this connection between sonship and image bearing quite clearly. "For those whom he foreknew he also pre-destined to be conformed to the image of his Son, in order that he might be the firstborn among many brethren" (Rom 8:29). God has made us image bearers so that he might have many sons alongside his unique Son, Jesus. Sonship is the restoration of the intimate Godward relationship of the image of God which was negativized by the fall. This should not surprise us because, as we have seen, the image of God is not some abstract attribute of man. It involves real relationships with God and other men. It is in our relationship to God as his children that we bear his image.

Renewed Relationships among Christians

This is not all. The same renewal of the image of God which makes us sons of God also makes us brethren of one another. The image of God has two facets—the Godward and the manward. They are not to be separated. Both the vertical and the horizontal relationships of the image of God were damaged by the fall; both are healed by the new creation in Christ.

Our role as brethren to one another restores the manward relationship. It is given to us right along with our role as children of

God—the restored Godward relationship. This is why Paul follows his exhortation to "put on the new nature, created after the likeness of God in true righteousness and holiness" (Eph 4:24), not by a call to be sons of God, but by instructions on proper human relationships. Consider this practical advice in Ephesians on how to live as brothers to one another:

Each of you must speak truth to his neighbor (v. 25)

Do not let the sun go down while you are still angry (v. 26)

Steal no longer (v. 28)

Work... (in order to) have something to share with those in need (v. 28)

Do not let any unwholesome talk come out of your mouths (v. 29)

Get rid of bitterness, rage, and anger, brawling and slander (v. 31)

Be kind and compassionate to one another, forgiving each other (v. 32)

This teaching about how to live with each other follows directly from Paul's exhortation to walk as image bearers of God. We are to act as a family because we are all made sons and daughters of God. We are brethren because we are made God's children. Our relationship with other men is restored along with our relationship with God. As Christians, we are all children of the same Father and should act as such. Our human relationships are no longer negativized. They are to be the positive, loving relationships of a family.

The re-creation of our vertical and horizontal relationships are not separate, but occur in the single act of new creation in Christ. John makes this abundantly clear when he says, "We know that we have passed from death to life, *because* we love the brethren" (1 Jn 3:14). For John, the visible horizontal relationships we have as brethren point to the invisible vertical relationship we have with God.

John returns to this concept over and over in his first epistle. Our visible horizontal relationships with other children of God express our invisible vertical relationship with the Father. Of course, John does not say that good horizontal relationships with other men will ever bring us into a vertical relationship with God. However, he does insist that our loving kinship with other Christians is an indispensible partner to our new loving relationship with God. The reverse is also true: "By this we know that we love the children of God, when we love God and obey his commandments" (1 Jn 5:2). Our renewed manward relationships flow directly from our renewed Godward relationship.

For the Christian, the vertical and horizontal relationships of the image of God are intertwined, for both our sonship and our brotherhood are accomplished in the same act of faith through which we came under Christ's headship. Thus we cannot have a super-spiritual gospel of experience of God without concrete practice of love for the brethren. Neither can we preach a social gospel without pointing to our transcendent relationship with God as his redeemed people. To separate the horizontal and vertical aspects of the image of God is less than biblical. Of course our position of sonship toward God does not mean that we become baby gods. To the contrary, in Christ we become truly human for the first time. We became something less than human when Adam rebelled against God. Now, through the new creation in Christ, we return to our true humanity as God's image bearers.

Indeed, this idea is the thrust of Ezekiel's prophecy about the new creation. The Lord says through him, "I will take out of your flesh the heart of stone and give you a heart of flesh" (Ez 36:26). When we are re-created in the image of God, we finally become who we are intended to be all along. In our insanity and rebellion we have lived with hearts "of stone." But when we enter into God's family we are given what we lost at the fall—hearts "of flesh," real human hearts. When we relate to God as Father and to his other children as brethren, we are finally human—true image bearers of God.

Let's ask our question again at this point: is Christian community biblical or optional? We can respond that it is. The answer is yes. Not only does it fit in with man's creation in the image of God, but it also fits the redemption we have in Christ. Although we have yet to see how Christian community might work out concretely, it is in harmony with these two basic biblical doctrines. The two-fold nature of Christian community — as *Christian* community (emphasizing our relationship with God) and Christian *community* (emphasizing our loving relationships as his children) — fits the pattern God has revealed concerning both the creation and new creation.

Accomplished-But-Not-Yet-Fulfilled

Through Christ's work, we have become a new humanity. This is an accomplished fact, finished on the cross. Yet there is a sense in which it is yet to come. As we have already seen, our state is "accomplished-but-not-yet-fulfilled." In Romans 8, Paul says that we "received [past tense] the spirit of sonship" (v. 15). A few verses later, Paul says that "we ourselves, who have the first fruits of the Spirit, groan inwardly as we *wait for adoption as sons, the redemption of our bodies*" (v. 23). We have already been adopted as sons, yet we still await our adoption as sons — specifically, the redemption of our bodies.

Our status as "accomplished-but-not-yet-fulfilled" is most obvious when we consider the renewal of our bodies. We bear the image of God as whole persons, and all parts of our being, including our bodies, are to be restored. Jesus' ministry of healing points toward the redemption of our bodies, and messianic prophecies like Isaiah 53:4 (cf. Mt 8:17) confirm that this is part of his plan. However, our complete physical renewal will occur in the future when the Lord returns.

It is because Paul is dealing with the nature of the resurrected body that he speaks in future terms of our re-creation in 1 Corinthians 15. His final description of our resurrection bodies is, "Just as we have borne the image of the man of dust [Adam], we shall also bear the image of the man of heaven [Christ]" (1 Cor 15:49). We will not "be like him" bodily until Christ returns.

Between the time of our rebirth in Jesus Christ and the time he returns to complete our renewal, we are called to live as the image bearers of God. This call is not an abstract theological category but a way of life. We are to live out our relationship with God as his children and our relationships to other believers as brethren in the present.

How are we to do this? What is the lifestyle of the image bearers of God? It can take many diverse forms. The loving relationships of God's image—toward God and toward one another—must have concrete reality in our day-to-day lives. To deal with the practicalities of living as God's image bearers, we must understand the context God has given us for bearing his image. That context is the church.

We could easily put together a long list of important practical aspects of image bearing. The New Testament is full of such teaching which we are to obey. However, we should avoid making such a list now because it might tend to make us conceive of the re-creation of the image of God in purely individualistic terms. Our question is always, "What does that mean *for me*?"

This would be a mistake. Bearing God's image is not purely an individualistic call. There is a sense in which God's redeemed family is to live out its redemption together. Because the church is our context for image bearing, there is a corporate aspect to living as image bearers of God. To understand what it means practically to be re-created in God's image, we must first consider how the people of God, the church, bear the image of God together.

Part Two

*Christian Community
and the Church*

THREE

COMMUNION
AND COMMUNITY

I HAVE long suspected that something funny is going on in American Christianity. For some years now, I've been taking an unofficial poll among people I meet, and have found that most of them are interested in religion but relatively few are interested in any external expression of that religion. "After all," they say, "religion is a personal matter."

Lately, the Gallup Poll, which is much more methodical about the public opinion business than I am, has confirmed my suspicion. Gallup says that a whopping 80 percent of Americans believe that "Jesus Christ was God or Son of God." When I read that, I said to myself, "Well, the United States certainly has a lot of orthodox people." The poll went on to say that 84 percent pray at least once a day. Apparently, Americans are not just orthodox people, but are relatively religious, orthodox people. But the poll also said that 41 percent (presumably including quite a few of these relatively religious, orthodox people) very seldom attend a church, and that even most of those who do (70 percent) think that church attendance is unimportant.

Apparently, religion is indeed "a personal matter" for Americans.

The evangelical movement in America has emphasized—rightly I think—that salvation is a matter of personal confrontation with God and conversion. "Unless one is born anew, he cannot see the kingdom of God" (Jn 3:3). This can only happen to one individual at a time, and is "a personal matter" in the most profound sense. Much of the beauty of God's love for man is seen in personal salvation; God does not just love mankind in general, he loves *me* personally. His love is not a philosophical abstraction; it's an intensely personal reality.

However, there is a danger inherent in this emphasis on the personal nature of salvation. While it is true that salvation is *individual*, it is certainly not *individualistic*. We tend to fall into a "me and Jesus" mentality that ignores the centrality of relationships and ministries among Christians. Some 70 percent of the people who go to church say that the church—the body of believers in Christ—is an unimportant thing. We have used our idea of a personal relationship with God as an excuse for doing whatever we please, without being responsible to or involved deeply with anyone.

This individualistic frame of mind bears little resemblance to the attitude of the apostles. Whenever Paul—or any other apostle—preached, he didn't just "save souls" and then say, "Well, you're going to go to heaven, see you then." Wherever he went he called people to a relationship with God by faith, and then brought them into churches where they could be built together with other Christians. The apostles had very good reasons for bringing the people who received their message into churches: God is not interested only in redeemed persons, but also in having a redeemed people. God's desire from the beginning has been to have "a kingdom of priests and a holy nation" (Ex 19:6), and this is precisely what he does have in his church (Rv 1:6; 1 Pt 2:9).

God's interest in a redeemed people means that salvation is not just individual; it has a corporate aspect as well. The corporate aspect of salvation finds expression as Christians come together in the church. The church as God's people is not to be thought of as a building on a street corner, or as a highly select social club. Rather, it is a group of people who have a corporate identity. In a real sense, a church is *one* entity, not just a collection of individuals. We saw this idea of corporate identity previously in Paul's concept of the two Adams. Before we were reborn, our corporate identity was in the clan of Adam. Now, however, we are in the tribe of Christ. We have a real solidarity with one another as members of the same tribe under our federal head. In fact, our identity with Christ is so close that it is not enough to call us his tribe; the scriptures speak of us as his "body."

The Individual and the Corporate

The metaphor of the body of Christ clearly brings out the idea that the church has a corporate identity made up of. diverse individuals. The church has many members, but it is only *one* body (1 Cor 12:12). The church is made up of many people, but it is only "*one* new man" (Eph 2:14-15). Our salvation involves not only coming into a relationship with Christ, but also coming into relationships with other believers in the church. This twofold direction of salvation parallels the vertical and horizontal aspects of the image of God which we bear in our relationships. In fact, the church is the context God has designed where his image is to be borne.

In the twentieth century, we are caught up in an individualistic view of salvation. Most people's attitudes toward the corporate aspect of salvation range from benign neglect to violent denial. Whenever anyone says that there is something to being a Christian besides our personal relationship with the Lord, many feel threatened and want to run. I have talked to person after person about the importance of corporate identity as the body of Christ and many of them vigorously deny it. I recall telling one woman that the group I was gathered with that night was a church with a common life together in Christ. She said, "No you're not—you're just a voluntary fellowship of individual believers." Nothing I could do would convince her otherwise. As far as she was concerned, the Christian life consisted of nothing but the individual's new relationship to God.

A Christian's individual life before God is of great importance, but it is simply not all there is to the Christian life. The individual nature of salvation is a biblical truth, and we have every right to emphasize it. But it is tragically wrong to use the biblical truth of the individual aspect of salvation to battle against the biblical truth of the corporate aspect of salvation. When we deny the corporate expression of our salvation in the church, we are essentially promoting the "doing-your-own-thing-ism" so prevalent in our society to the status of biblical Christianity. Unfortunately, this is using our own cultural biases to deny the teaching of scripture. This cultural bias against the corporate identity of the church has two roots, both of which run deeply into our patterns of life and thought.

One root of our bias against corporate identity is our heritage from the Renaissance of the concept of "autonomous man." The idea that man is autonomous (which literally means "self-law" or "self-centered") takes the biblical understanding of the dignity of each person to such an extreme that relationships between persons are of little importance. It states that all that matters is that the individual be unhindered in exercising his individuality. This attitude is common in our society. People "drop out," leaving behind wives, children, and families in pursuit of "freedom." Their responsibilities in relationship with other persons are of little concern. All that matters is that the individual be able to do whatever he wants whenever he wants. These people are seeking personal fulfillment at any cost, disregarding their responsibilities to others.

The same attitude surfaces in a less hideous manner in our modern ideal of success—the self-made man. Our culture thinks that the person who really deserves our respect is the one who started with nothing and made himself important with no one else's help. A logical extension of this attitude is seen in the recent rash of bestsellers telling people how to succeed in life by asserting themselves and stepping on others. If I am the only one who really matters, I'd better try to "make it" in life, no matter what damage it does to those around me. This is a long way from the biblical teaching to "outdo one another in showing honor" (Rom 12:10), but it fits well with man's desire to "be like God." The origins of the autonomous individualism of the self-made man with its emphasis on self-sufficiency are found in the disaster of the fall, not in God's way of working with us.

The second root of our bias against the corporate aspect of Christianity is our aversion to communism. By and large, there is a terrible devastation of the individual person in the world's communist societies. To achieve the goal of a "classless society," the state strips the individual of personal rights. Because the person is virtually meaningless apart from his context in society, his dignity as an individual human being vanishes. This is why it is important to emphasize that the corporate aspect of our salvation exists within the structure of personalness. We must keep in mind the fact that the identity of the individual is stressed, not lost, in this corporate structure. Each person is meaningful in himself as a creature before God. Yet God has not created us to be individuals only, but also to be in relationship with one another in the corporate context of the church.

Indeed, the place where communist society and the church stand most sharply opposed is precisely over the role of the individual within the corporate identity. A communist society is *collective*; it sees itself as made up of many individuals who are essentially interchangeable units. Thus the individual loses his identity, for he is no different than anyone else. All are merely parts of the huge social organism. The individual can take his meaning only from the organism, since its parts are meaningful only in terms of the larger whole.

The church, however, is not *collective* by nature, but is *corporate*. The parts are not identical but are "members [literally, 'organs'] of the body" of Christ (1 Cor 12:12-30). Each "organ" is unique and retains its individuality, but all function together as one body. The individual is not lost in the corporate identity of the church, but is freed to function as who he really is, for as each individual functions in the body, he will bear the vertical and horizontal relationships of the image of God.

The key to the corporate nature of the church is that something more than just the sum of the individual members is involved as the church functions. Jesus said, "Where two or three are gathered in my name, there am I in the midst of them" (Mt 18:20). Notice that he did not say "Where *one* is gathered in my name..." When the people of God come together, Christ is present in a way in which he is not present for the individual alone. This is a special event: Though Christ abides in each of us individually, when we come together he is in our midst uniquely. Part of this uniqueness is, as we will see, that the church in its corporate identity bears the image of God.

The Church as a Living Thing

The word that our New Testament translations render as "church" (Greek, *ekklesia*) denoted, in its general usage, a political gathering. The New Testament uses the word once in this sense, to describe a public assembly at Ephesus (Acts 19:32). However, the Christians derived their meaning of the word not from this political usage but from the Septuagint translation of the Old Testament which used *ekklesia* to describe the assembly of God's people Israel. In the New Testament writings, *ekklesia* came to mean the assembly of God's people, both Jews and Gentiles. When we read "church" in the Bible, we must always keep in mind that this describes an assembly of *people* who call the Lord their God. The modern idea that the church is a building is foreign to New Testament usage. There the church is always a group of God's *people*, never a building.

The description of God's people as his "church" is applied in a limited number of ways in scripture. Its broadest application is to the totality of all believers everywhere—the universal or catholic church (Col 1:18, 24; Eph 1:22; 3:10). It also describes all Christians in a given locality such as the Galatian region (Gal 1:2) or the city of Laodicea (Col 4:16). Some of these local "churches" were small enough to meet in a home (1 Cor 16:19). Churches such as the one in Priscilla and Aquila's home (Rom 16:5) apparently had an established identity within the larger city-wide church in Rome, even though they could hardly have been larger than twenty or so people.

Broadly speaking, then, the New Testament conceptualizes the church in two ways: as the universal church and as the local church. The local church may cover any convenient area—a province, a city, or a neighborhood—but even the smallest of these is really the church, not merely a portion of it. Paul did not greet "the part of the church" in Aquila and Priscilla's home. Even though only a few people were involved there, it was "the church" just as much as all the Christians in Rome were "the church." The smallest example of the church, the church in a home, still displays all essential characteristics of the largest example of the church, the church catholic.

It is important for our purposes to think in terms of small examples of the church, like the New Testament church in a home. If we think of the church as the universal, or even city-wide church in this discussion, we risk losing ourselves in abstractions. To understand the church as the image bearer of God, we need to conceptualize it on a scale we can make practical. How can we practice Jesus' command that those who follow him should love each other as he loved us—that is, sacrificially (Jn 15:12)? How can we love the millions in the universal church or even the hundreds in the city-wide church in such a deep sense? These things are beyond the realities of our day-to-day lives.

It is possible, though, to begin to love a group of people small enough to fit in a house and to love them in a self-giving way. When we think in terms of small examples of the church, we have a better chance to put the realities which are to characterize the church into practice. Nothing is lost by conceptualizing the church in a small way, for even a church in a house is "the church" in the full sense, and not just a piece of it. But much is gained by this method, for a small model of the church makes it possible for us to integrate some important truths into our lives on a scale we can make practical.

Even the smallest imaginable cohesive group of Christians—where two or three are gathered in Christ's name—is still "the church." It displays all the characteristics of the church because Christ is uniquely in their midst. One of these characteristics which belongs to every assembly of God's people, regardless of size, is *life*. Each church on the New Testament model has an observable life of its own. It can truly be thought of as a vital organism instead of a dead thing.

The quality of life in the church is well illustrated by the metaphors which scripture applies to it. It is called a "spiritual house" made up of "living stones" (1 Pt 2:5; cf. Eph 2:20-22; Heb 3:6), a building which is not inorganic but "growing" (Eph 2:21). The church is a "flock" (1 Pt 5:2), the "bride of Christ" (Rv 21:2, 9), God's family (Eph 2:19), and many other things. Running through all these figures is a concept of the church as a vital organism, never static, never dead.

The Church and the Image of God

Of all the biblical pictures of the church, the one which portrays its life in the most striking way is the concept of the church as the "body of Christ" (Rom 12:3-8; 1 Cor 12:12-31; Eph 4:11-16; Col 1:18, 24). The concept of the "bodyhood" of the church runs through Paul's letters. It is one of his basic categories for understanding its nature.

Briefly, the idea is that the church should function like the human body. The body is a single organism, but it is made up of many different parts, each of which has a specific function. Each part is specifically equipped for its own function (eyes for seeing, ears for hearing), but the whole body operates as a unity and Christ directs it as its head. Thus, the body of Christ, the church, is one living entity made up of many members, each of which is intimately involved in the vitality of the whole.

To deal with our main concern—the church as the image bearer of God—we need to focus on one curious aspect of Paul's idea of the bodyhood of the church. In 1 Corinthians 12, his most detailed expression of the body of Christ metaphor, Paul introduces his teaching by saying, "For just as the body [that is, the human body] is one and has many members, and all the members of the body, though many, are one body, *so it is with Christ*" (1 Cor 12:12). One would have expected Paul to say, "*so it is with the church,*" for his point is that the church is one organism made up of many parts. But he does say, "*so it is with Christ,*" deliberately making a quasi-identification between the church as Christ's body and Christ himself. Why did he do this?

Of course, the church and Christ are by no means the same thing: The church is the bride, Christ is the bridegroom; the church is the spiritual house where God dwells, not God himself. Since Paul would not confuse Christ the Savior with the church of the saved, there must be another meaning to his teaching about the body of Christ. The quasi-identification of Christ with his church is our first indication that something much deeper than a metaphor is involved in the bodyhood of the church.

Paul may intend this same kind of quasi-identification of Christ and the church when he writes about "the mystery of Christ"

(Rom 11:25; Eph 3:4, 6; Col 1:25-28). "The mystery of Christ" is that, under the New Covenant, the Gentiles and not only the Jews are part of the people of God, the church. Paul could have just as easily called this "the mystery of the church." Instead, he called it "the mystery of Christ," thereby heightening his quasi-identification of Christ and the church. As he puts it, "This mystery is that through the gospel the Gentiles are heirs together in the promise in Christ Jesus" (Eph 3:6). The key to these seeming identifications of the church with Christ lies in the bodyhood of the church, for if the church is Christ's body, it should resemble him. The two can be placed in these conjunctions because the church should look like Christ.

Because the church looks like Christ, Paul looked *beyond* the action of the church as a body to the actions of Christ who is the head. When the church functioned as a body, Paul saw Christ, not because the church *is* Christ, but because the church bears the image of God and so *looks like* Christ. The apostle's vision for the church was the same as that for each believer—to see "Christ formed in you" (Gal 4:19). Both the individual and the church are to bear God's image.

The same concept of the church as the image bearer of God underlies Ephesians 2:11-22, where Paul expresses another facet of the uniqueness of the church. Here he says that Christ has broken down the division and hatred between Jews and Gentiles so that he could "create *in himself one new man* in place of the two, so making peace" (Eph 2:15). The "one new man" which Christ created "in himself" at the cross is the expression of the beginning of the new creation.

There is a corporate dimension to the new creation just as there was a corporate dimension to the fall when we all sinned as a "result of the one man's sin" (Rom 5:16). We are individually re-created to be image bearers of God. But corporately we are re-created together into "one new man," the church, who bears Christ's image.

Paul sees the church in categories much like those applied to the individual as God's image bearer. This is clear in his discussion in Ephesians 2 of the consequences of his creation of one new man. This one new man binds Jews and Gentiles together into proper horizontal relationships as brethren in "the household of God" (v. 19). It also builds the two groups together into a proper vertical relationship with God as "a holy temple in the Lord" (vv. 20-22). The proper manward and Godward relationships which characterize the image of God are both obvious here. In the "one new man," proper human relationships are renewed as the barriers between us are destroyed (vv. 14, 16, 17, 19), and we are brought into a proper relationship with God as his worshipers (vv. 16, 18, 20-22). Thus, the church is called corporately to display the proper horizontal relationships of the image of God, just as we are called to display them individually.

Thus our role as God's image bearers is not individualistic in nature, but involves both individual and corporate expressions of the proper relationships of his image. We must uphold the value and integrity of every individual as God's image bearer. But we dare not be trapped into an individualism which denies the corporate image of God in his church. The church is the sphere God has designed for his image—both individual and corporate—to be displayed. It is the context he has given us for bearing the image of God.

A Reconciled People

As the context of our image bearing, the church stands as the primary expression on earth of God's new creation. We are each re-created as God's image bearer and, as one new man, we bear his image corporately in the church. However, our re-creation as image bearers is not the end of the matter. God's goal is the renewal of the entire creation (Rom 8:19-22) in the ultimate "summing up of all things in Christ" (Eph 1:10). Our renewal in his image is the first part of this program, but it will only be completed when every knee bows at the highly exalted name of Jesus (Phil 2:9-11).

Paul expresses God's goal of "summing up all things in Christ" in the midst of his great hymn of praise in Colossians 1.

(Christ) is the head of the body, the church; he is the beginning and the firstborn from among the dead, so that in everything he might have the supremacy. For God was pleased to have all his fullness dwell in him, *and through him to reconcile to himself all things*, whether things on earth or things in heaven, by making peace through his blood, shed on the cross.

Once you were alienated from God and were enemies in your minds because of your evil behavior. *But now he has reconciled you by Christ's physical body through death* to present you holy in his sight, without blemish and free from accusation. (Col 1:18-22)

The "summing up of all things in Christ" is based on his work on the cross, where he made peace. This peace is peace with God for men who were "once alienated from God and were enemies" (v. 21). We had been fighting a war of rebellion against our Creator, but peace was made at the cross, and we have been reconciled to God through Christ's death (v. 22). However, this re-creation of a proper relationship between God and men — the central meaning of "reconciliation" — is only the beginning of God's ultimate goal: "to reconcile to himself all things" (v. 20).

God's ultimate goal of reconciling all things to himself is another aspect of his working which is "accomplished-but-not-yet-fulfilled." Our reconciliation, and the reconciliation of "all things," was finished on the cross, but its fulfillment is yet to come. Creation is still "subjected to futility" (Rom 8:20) as a result of the fall. We still await the redemption of our bodies, certainly part of our reconciliation, but a part not yet fulfilled. However, our reconciliation has been accomplished. It has brought us into a relationship of sonship with God as his image bearers, so we can stand before him as his children "without blemish and free from accusation" (v. 22).

The peace Christ made for us on the cross is a two-fold peace, a peace both with God and with men. Paul summarizes his teaching on justification by saying, "Therefore, since we are justified by faith, *we have peace with God* through our Lord Jesus Christ... For if while we were enemies *we were reconciled to God* by the death of his Son, much more, *now that we are reconciled*, shall we be saved by his life" (Rom 5:1, 10). The peace on the cross is an end to our war with God, for our relationship with him has been changed from that of enemies to that of sons. Christ, at the cross, *reconciled* us to God, making peace.

Christ also brought peace to our wars with other men. "For *he is our peace*, who has made us both [Jews and Gentiles] one, and has broken down the dividing wall of hostility...that he might create in himself one new man in place of the two, *so making peace*" (Eph 2:14, 15). The hostile manner in which we conduct our human relationships was epitomized for Paul by the fighting between Jews and Gentiles. Even this hard-core racial hatred has been destroyed by the peace established on the cross. Thus the peace which Christ has brought to our negativized vertical and horizontal relationships is at the core of the reconciliation he has accomplished. Because we have been reconciled, a fundamental change has taken place in the way we conduct our personal relationships with God and other persons. The image of God has been re-created.

The Ministry of Reconciliation

In 2 Corinthians, Paul takes up the topic of reconciliation again, but this time with an important extension.

> Therefore, if any one is in Christ, *he is a new creation*; the old has passed away, behold, the new has come. All this is from God, who through *Christ reconciled us to himself* and *gave us the ministry of reconciliation;* that is, God was in Christ reconciling the world to himself, not counting their trespasses against them, and entrusting to us the message of reconciliation. So we are ambassadors for Christ, God making his appeal through us. We beseech you on behalf of Christ, be *reconciled to God.* (2 Cor 5:17-20)

Not only have we been reconciled, but we have also been given "the ministry of reconciliation." We are called, as the first part of God's new creation, to minister reconciliation to those around us.

This means that God has given us an active role in the ultimate fulfillment of his desire of "summing up all things in Christ" by committing to us "the message of reconciliation" (v. 19). When we read this we tend to think that it means we are to preach the gospel. This is true, but that is not all it means. Paul's mind was not compartmentalized like the modern mind. For him, the "message of reconciliation" we preach to the world is to be expressed in our words *and* our actions, not in our words alone. The ministry of reconciliation includes preaching the good news, but the word of reconciliation is spoken by the totality of our lives as God's children.

Why else would Paul exhort the Corinthians to "be reconciled to God" (v. 20)? These people were already professing Christians; why should he tell them to be reconciled to God? The problem was not that they needed to be "born again" again; but that they were not acting out their reconciliation in deeds with their words.

Exactly which issue at Corinth evoked this plea to be reconciled to God is not clear. It probably concerned their near rejection of Paul's apostleship and thus a near rejection of God's ministry through him. In any case, the outcome in Paul's eyes was that their behavior was not in line with the reconciliation God had accomplished in them. In order for the word of reconciliation to bear good fruit, it must be acted out as well as spoken.

A similar concept of ministry was in Jesus' mind when he prayed just before his arrest: "I do not pray for these only [the Twelve], but also for those who are to believe in me through their word, that they may all be one...*so that the world may believe that thou hast sent me*" (Jn 17:20-21; cf., vv. 23, 26). Our Lord's prayer here is striking: The world will believe that Jesus came from the Father on the basis of the loving unity among Christians. Reconciled human relationships are an integral part of the message of reconciliation. Our visible preaching by means of loving actions gives empirical evidence that our verbal preaching is true and not merely another empty philosophy.

Demonstration and Proclamation

Visible preaching of the word of reconciliation is especially important today. Modern men are infatuated with the scientific method as an empirical way of verifying facts. Many are under the impression that empirical evidence is the ultimate test of truth. Although Christians cannot accept that view, we are in an excellent position to give the world the empirical evidence it considers so important. As ministers of reconciliation, we not only preach the gospel but also give empirical evidence of its truth through our lives.

The message of reconciliation involves both the verbal and the visible spheres. One without the other is woefully inadequate. If we give just a verbal witness, without any visible evidence in our lives that our witness is true, we are hypocrites. Not only do we not "practice what we preach," but we turn it into a lie. Though we say that what we believe is important, we live as though it were inconsequential. We are like people running through the streets without raincoats, yelling, "It's going to rain." People will look at us and reply, "If you're so sure it's going to rain, why aren't you dressed for it?" And they'll ignore our message. Our verbal proclamation must have with it a visible demonstration in order to be effective.

On the other hand, a visible message of reconciliation without the verbal aspect is also inadequate. The world is full of nice guys. What ultimately distinguishes a Christian nice guy from an agnostic nice guy or from a Hindu nice guy? Although we could argue about many possible differences, the only *radical* difference is the message of faith and salvation in Jesus Christ. We cannot expect people to read between the lines of our lives and deduce the full-orbed Christian message. Rather, we must correlate our visible demonstration with a verbal proclamation.

This verbal proclamation need not be an eloquent, dynamic sermon. God has not seen fit to gift every member of the body of Christ with a golden tongue. Our proclamation can be something as simple and homespun as, "I'm the way I am because Jesus has made peace with God for me," or, "I called on God and he saved me." This is what Peter meant when he said, "Always be prepared to make a defense to any one who calls you to account for the hope that is in you" (1 Pt 3:15). The point is not that every Christian should preach beautiful sermons to all his friends, but rather that we should be able to tell people in a simple and straightforward manner why we are the way we are.

The verbal proclamation and the visible demonstration are so closely united that it is best to look at them as two sides of the same coin. The verbal explains the visible and visible gives evidence to the truth of the verbal. Our attitude should be like Paul's when he said, "My message and my preaching were not with wise and persuasive words [the verbal alone is not enough] but with a demonstration of the Spirit's power" (1 Cor 2:4). What is this "demonstration of the Spirit's power?" Did it consist *only* of raising the dead or some other dramatic manifestation of God's power? Or are there also other more subtle ways in which we are called to demonstrate the power of the God whom we proclaim?

The demonstration of the message of reconciliation to the world requires two things. First, we must practically live out our reconciliation with God (2 Cor 5:19). Second, we must live in practical reconciliation with the other children in God's family. By showing ourselves to be reconciled to both God and man, we demonstrate the power and validity of the gospel.

The first aspect of our reconciliation—our reconciliation with God—must be a constant feature of our lives. It does little good to say God is our Father and then only pay attention to him once a week. How does God act as our Father when we make our life decisions without even consulting him? How can we live as children of God when we rely on him for getting us to heaven and rely on ourselves for everything else?

Let's take saying "grace" before meals as an example. It is an appropriate and honorable thing to return thanks to God for the food we eat, because it really does come from his hand. However, these special times of thanksgiving are not to be the only times we remember the Lord in the midst of an entire day. Rather, they are the times when we do in a concentrated way that which we do throughout our lives—namely, giving thanks to our good Father for his good gifts. Scripture's injunction to "rejoice *always*, pray *constantly*, give thanks in *all* circumstances" (1 Thes 5:16-18) needs to be increasingly the manner of our lives, for we have been reconciled to God. We should live our lives thanking God not just for the food we eat, but for the water we drink and the air we breathe! God is providing us with all we need at every instant of our lives. Because we are reconciled with him, we are to live as his children—seeking his guidance, accepting his provision, and loving and worshipping him as a way of life.

The second aspect of our visible demonstration is to live in practical reconciliation with the other children in God's family. John said, "He who says he is in the light and hates his brother is in the darkness still" (1 Jn 2:9). Jesus' prayer in John 17 makes love among Christians mandatory. A part of the message we preach to the world will inevitably include the way we carry out our human relationships in the church.

If we are aloof or unloving in our relationships in the church, why should the world not dismiss the gospel of Christ as merely another religion? Jesus himself gave them that privilege (Jn 17:23). I know a number of people who looked into Christianity, and then decided that it was a lot of nonsense because they found Christians to be self-righteous and condemning rather than loving with each other. When things like this happen we should not give up hope, but rather treat it as a call from God for our repentance.

We will be imperfect both in the way we love God, and in the way we love each other, for we still live in a fallen order. The perfection of God is simply not available to us. Nonetheless, we need to ask God continually to renew us and to show in the present the reconciliation he has accomplished in our lives.

God has called us to be clouded mirrors of his character. He has not seen fit to make us perfect in this life, but he has given us the grace to be faithful as earthen vessels which contain the vast treasure of Christ's life (2 Cor 4:7). After all, God himself has called us to demonstrate the message of reconciliation; he will surely give us the grace to carry out that demonstration.

Because God has called us this way, our role is to live out the substantial renewal of the image of God which Christ accomplished. The world needs to see that we bear God's image in our horizontal and vertical relationships. Image bearing is the visible part of the "message of reconciliation" which we are to preach and demonstrate. A theological category is not sufficient in itself, for our role as the image bearers of God cannot be merely talked about. It must also be lived.

The church is the environment God has designed for the display of his image, and there is a sense in which the church bears this image corporately. Thus, our individual and corporate demonstrations of the image of God will coalesce in the context of the church. As we function together in the body of Christ we will bear God's image primarily in two ways: vertically through worship and horizontally through community.

In the vertical dimensions, Christians are called, both corporately and individually, to be worshippers of God. Our renewed relationship with him should break forth into worship and praise. Formerly we were his enemies, haters of God, and set on being self-sufficient. The re-creation he has carried out in us has changed us into creatures who know that their chief end is to "worship God and enjoy him forever" (Westminster Catechism). As we live a life of thanksgiving to God, we will bear his image in a way the world desperately needs to see. We will consider this vertical aspect of image bearing later, but we need to keep it in mind in the meantime because our horizontal relationships with other Christians flow directly from our relationship with our Father.

God also calls us to display his image horizontally in what we will here call "community." Community with other Christians does not necessarily mean living together (communalism) or even residing in the same neighborhood, although either may be involved. At the core of the community is an acting out of the caring relationships of a family, for we are all sons and daughters of the same Father. Community means *being* the church.

In the community of the church, the re-created horizontal relationships of the image of God are brought into reality both individually and corporately. The world desperately needs to see these kinds of caring relationships among Christians in the context of the worshipping church. In the following chapters we will consider the expression of the horizontal relationships of the image of God first, and move from there to the expression of the vertical relationship with God which brings them into being.

FOUR

THE FELLOWSHIP OF
THE HOLY SPIRIT

HE late 60's and early 70's saw one of the most widespread
outbreaks of community-building that American society
has ever witnessed. From the "hippie" communes to the
"straight" alternative religious and social communities, people
from every segment of our culture sought different ways of living
together. Why were so many people, both young and old, looking
for a new way of living?

Although the answers to this question varied widely, a typical
response ran something like this: "Our society is unhealthy. We
are bombarded by advertisers who create needs for their products.
We have meaningless jobs that make work seem unending, yet
nothing seems to last — washing machines, presidents, cars, and
friendships all seem to have obsolescence built into them from the
start. Worst of all, the relationships in our lives — our marriages,
families, and associations — are superficial. No one wants to know
anyone else deeply. We feel alone in a faceless crowd."

There can be little doubt that many people living in mass societies like the United States experience an almost desperate need
for community. Because our culture does not satisfy this need for
intimate, lasting human relationships, some who feel the need
most intensely are willing to try almost any experiment which
gives them hope of attaining some measure of community. Some
of these experiments succeed, most fail, but all testify to the importance of community to human beings.

One of the tragic aspects of this modern search for community has been that the church has largely ignored it. Except for some scattered groups along its fringe, the American church has been quite content to continue functioning in the model it has evolved over the past few decades. According to this model the truly successful church is one with thousands of members and one which freely uses Madison Avenue advertising techniques in its preaching and evangelism. In short, the successful church has mimicked the mass society. The successful church is the "mass church."

However, the "mass church," like the mass society, has no way to meet the human need for community. It might try programs and structures such as encounter groups or weekend retreats to encourage people to stop being superficial with one another. However, these are half-measures at best. People generally change right back to the superficial way of relating until the next retreat comes along. Such an intermittent approach to community forces people to look elsewhere for the reconciled relationships they should find in the church.

It has always been recognized that the church is to be a sphere of reconciliation for human relationships, and that this recon ciliation is to be not just an absence of hatred but a presence of love such that the church lives as one new man. Unfortunately, this ideal has seldom been worked out consistently in practice. Usually, the only time proper personal relationships are considered is in the sphere of some external moral code. Love is seen only in terms of a legal morality, a set of do's and don't's. "The fellowship of the Holy Spirit" (2 Cor 13:14) is relegated to a mystical oneness in the heavenlies that has little concrete reality in the present life. It should come as no surprise that the unbelieving world is no longer shocked into saying, "How these Christians love one another!" as it was in the early third century.

By devaluing community and making "the fellowship of the Holy Spirit" insubstantial in the present life, we have missed the full joy and healing to be experienced in a church which "turned the world upside down." The tragic thing is that our loss has not only been personal. Because of our lack of love for one another, we have made the ministry of reconciliation ineffective. Jesus gave the world the privilege of knowing that the Father sent him into the world based on our love and unity as Christians. He considered it to be essential for his followers to be a true community in the eyes of the world. We have the right doctrines and put much energy into preaching the gospel, but we are undeniably guilty of the great error of the modern church — lack of community. No wonder the world doesn't listen.

This great error will not be corrected merely by changing methods or programs, although this must happen. Along with these external changes, our attitudes must be reshaped by the Holy Spirit to match the attitudes toward community seen in the apostolic church. As Francis Schaeffer has said, we must have an "orthodoxy of community" alongside our orthodoxy of doctrine.

The model for our orthodoxy of community must be the apostolic church. This does not mean that we should absolutize the forms adopted by the church in any time, even in the first century. However, the apostolic church is our model because the living apostles, men trained by the Lord Jesus himself, were directing the community life we find outlined in Acts and in the Epistles. We may or may not want to adopt the same practical expressions of community that they did, but we do need to adopt the attitudes and understandings of men who walked with the Lord. Thus, we shall examine Acts first. We shall try to determine how the apostles understood Christian community, and how this understanding worked out in practice for the churches under their guidance.

The Importance of Acts 1-12

When he wrote Acts, Luke was by his own declaration acting as a historian (Lk 1:1-3; Acts 1:1-2). He set out to sift the great wealth of data before him and put it into a meaningful form. His purpose was not merely to record raw facts in an unrelated and detached manner. But neither was he a novelist of rare genius who made up a vivid, though fictitious, account of Christian beginnings. As a historian, Luke wrote Acts by carefully choosing and accurately recording certain historical events to give a portrait of the early church and the people who composed it. The emphases in his picture can give us great insight into how the apostolic church acted out its true nature as one new man.

Luke's portrait of the early church has two distinct but inter-related parts: the community in Jerusalem (chapters 1-12) and the missionary journeys of Paul (chapters 13-28). The first part deals with the establishment and growth of the church at Jerusalem and with the inclusion of both the Samaritans and Gentiles in its ever-widening sphere. The main character is Peter, spokesman for the twelve apostles. Paul's ministry is related to the function of the Jerusalem church through his introduction in 8:1-3 and his conversion in 9:1-30. Paul does not replace Peter as the focus of Luke's interest until he tells of Paul's various missions, beginning in chapter 13.

Luke's attention to the Jerusalem church is significant. Luke was Paul's traveling companion, and his main concern in Acts seems to be with Paul's ministry. However, he spends nearly half of his book dealing with Jerusalem. Luke also must have had difficulty documenting the story of the Jerusalem church. The historical information about Paul was readily available to him. He could have quizzed the apostle at length during their travels together. By contrast, Luke probably had to do a lot of inves-tigative work to gather the necessary data to write about the Jerusalem church. Thus the very fact that Luke spent the time and effort necessary to write extensively about the Jerusalem church in Acts 1-12 makes it clear that what happened there is essential to our understanding of Paul's missions. That story in Acts 1-12 might be summed up under the heading, "Establish-ment of the Community."

The Great Jerusalem Commune?

The story begins with the giving of the Holy Spirit on Pentecost. There was an important difference between the Spirit's ministry under the Old Covenant given at Sinai and the New Covenant given on Pentecost. Under the Sinai covenant, the Holy Spirit was given to only a few of God's people—chiefly prophets, priests, and kings—who were functioning in an official capacity in Israel's theocracy. Under the New Covenant, the Holy Spirit is

poured out on all God's people. This was made obvious on
Pentecost when something like a great wind filled the room where
the disciples were. Flames of fire appeared above their heads, and
soon they came rushing into the crowded street speaking excitedly
in languages they had never learned (Acts 2:1-4).

These events must have surprised the pious crowd outside who
were on their way to the temple for the Pentecost services. The
onlookers had two initial reactions to these excited, obviously
uneducated Galileans speaking fluently in other languages. Some
were amazed but bewildered by what they heard; others decided
they were listening to a bunch of drunkards (vv. 5-13). In order to
resolve the confusion and explain this unprecedented occurrence,
Peter quotes Joel's prophecy, "I will pour out my Spirit upon all
flesh" (2:17).

One of the most striking themes in Joel's prophecy is the universality of the Spirit's ministry. He will be poured out on "all flesh,"
"your sons and daughters," "young men," "old men," "both men
and women." On Pentecost, the monopoly of the adult Jewish
male in ministry to the Lord was permanently broken, for the
"one new man" was born. In this one new man, "There is neither
Jew nor Greek, slave nor free, male nor female" (Gal 3:28). This
did not mean that God made his people impersonally interchangeable. Rather, it meant that they were one as God's
children and partakers of his Spirit.

Peter's sermon continues with his eyewitness attestation of
Jesus' death, resurrection, and ascension, and concludes with a
call to repent, be baptized, and receive the Holy Spirit promised
in Joel's prophecy. "The promise is to you and to your children
[the Jews]," says Peter, "and to all that are far off [Gentiles],
every one whom the Lord our God calls to him" (Acts 2:39).

Luke reports that about three thousand people heeded Peter's
call to repentance and baptism, but he does not say anything explicitly concerning the outpouring of the Spirit on them. What he
does do is spend verses 42-47 recording the result of the Holy
Spirit's work in one long sentence.

And they devoted themselves to the apostles' teaching *and*
fellowship, to the breaking of bread *and* the prayers. *And* fear

came upon every soul; *and* many wonders *and* signs were done through the apostles. *And* all who believed were together *and* had all things in common; *and* they sold their possessions and goods *and* distributed them to all, as any had need. *And* day by day, attending the temple together *and* breaking bread in their homes, they partook of food with glad and generous hearts, praising God *and* having favor with all the people. *And* the Lord added to their number day by day those who were being saved. (Acts 2:42-47)

No matter how we punctuate these verses for ease of reading, the fourteen "and's" make Luke's point clear: All these things are the one result of salvation and the outpouring of the Spirit (v. 40). For these first Christians, salvation was not just a warm feeling inside, but a lifestyle which encompassed every facet of their beings.

The overall impression left by these verses is that the Jerusalem Christians were seldom out of each other's sight. They ate together (v. 46), went to the temple together (v. 46), listened to the apostles' teaching together (v. 42). In fact, Luke says they did just about everything except sleep together. Their unity was so great that foreigners (vv. 9-11) who were certainly among those who believed apparently did not rush back to their hometowns, but instead stayed in the Jerusalem community. Many even sold some of their property to help meet the material needs of other believers (v. 45).

Some people treat this "communal" aspect of the Jerusalem church as a colossal mistake. As far as we know, the practice of selling individual property and sharing the proceeds was not carried on outside the first church. Apart from the first twelve chapters of Acts, the Bible is silent concerning the fate of "The Great Jerusalem Commune." Some, arguing from this silence of the scriptures, see these verses as a description of an incipient communism which the apostles, seeing their error, later quashed. Things were moving too fast for the Twelve to keep up, so these interpreters say, and they recognized the folly of the communal format of church life only after years of hard experience.

Interpretations such as these rest on preconceived notions

about the relationship between Christianity and personal property which are read *into* the text, not *out of* it. For his part, Luke goes out of his way to show that "The Great Jerusalem Commune," far from being a mistake, was one of the most praiseworthy results of the first outpouring of the Spirit, even if it did have its drawbacks.

He comes back to the practice again in Acts 5 in the story of Annanias and Sapphira. They were struck dead for duplicity when they brought to the apostles only a part of the price of their liquidated property, claiming that it was the full price. Even as late as Acts 6, some if not all of the church members were still eating together daily. At every turn, Luke speaks of these practices in the most glowing terms, describing them more as a pinnacle of success than a gross error.

Community in the Jerusalem Church

Before we can understand Luke's positive attitude toward "The Great Jerusalem Commune," we need to clear up two misconceptions about the way it functioned. First, it was not communism in the Marxist sense at all. Annanias was condemned not because he failed to bring all the proceeds of his land sale; it was his own personal property all along. He was condemned because he lied about the amount of the sale, wanting to appear "super-spiritual" to the rest of the church (Acts 5:1-4). In his case, and every other one recorded, the communalism in Jerusalem was based on free giving, not compulsion.

Second, the object of the sharing was not to make all members of the community equally wealthy. Its purpose was to help those who had real needs. There may well have been those in the church who remained wealthy, but "there was not a needy person among them" (Acts 4:34). The apostles had no intention of creating a classless society. They desired to see those whom the Lord had blessed materially share with those who had little.

The first Christians in Jerusalem had an attitude which is sadly lacking among most modern Christians: When they saw a need, they met it. Some of them may even have given their entire life savings to help those in need. In any case, they reacted to the situation of their brethren by sharing without counting the cost. The Jerusalem Christians saw the great importance of community in the Christian life and were willing to do whatever was needed to take part in it.

The attitudes of the first Christians are of even more interest to us than the actual format of community they adopted. Behind the selling of their property, we can see minds and hearts set on the importance of community. People were at work meeting the very real need of others in the community. When people were left with nothing to eat, they shared meals. When someone's sandals wore out, they got him new ones. There must have been dozens of such little "emergencies" each day. But in the Jerusalem church, they met each others' needs because they saw themselves as a community in which each acted as his brother's keeper.

The attitude toward community exemplified in Acts 2 was an enduring part of the life of the first Christians. The need for selling property and sharing the proceeds may have decreased over time, especially after many left Jerusalem following the persecution recorded in Acts 8. But it seems doubtful that the "communal" practices of the Jerusalem Church stopped because they were wrong or because the apostles disliked them. When they did stop, it was because they were no longer the best way of meeting the needs which existed in the church. The Christians' attitude of love and watch-care for the brethren took other forms, perhaps not quite as dramatic, but just as important. They recognized that their desire to care for one another was the practical result of God's grace (Acts 4:32-35).

It is quite easy to emphasize the material aspects of the community in Jerusalem because Luke emphasizes them, possibly because the sharing of goods was the most difficult thing for fallen, selfish people to do. Nonetheless, the community that the first Christians experienced was not *only* material; it affected virtually every sphere of their involvement with one another. For example, when Peter and John were released after their first confrontation with the Jewish high council, they went straight to the group of believers they were intimately associated with, and they all prayed about it "with one accord" (Acts 4:23-24). Or again, when Peter was thrown in jail (Acts 12:1-4), the church engaged in fervent prayer for him (v. 5). When he was miraculously set free, he went straight to the church, which was still praying for him (v. 12). Luke had events like these in mind when he described the congregation in Jerusalem as having "one heart and soul" (Acts 4:32).

The love the believers in Jerusalem had for one another was a love that was alive and worked to meet each other's needs. This care for one another was not only material or only spiritual, but it reached to all spheres of life. The Jerusalem church was not unique in these attitudes. As the first church, it formed the model for the other churches, sharing many features in common with them, including an overwhelming desire to minister to the needs of others and to base their lives as churches in their lives as communities.

Community in Paul's Churches

This attitude toward community also characterized the churches Paul planted. In the Gentile churches, this desire to act as "one new man" took different forms than in the mother church. It even extended in scope into the wider sphere of sharing with other communities. We can see this in the reaction of the Antioch church to Agabus' prophecy in Acts 11:27-30 that a great famine would come. In response, the brethren at Antioch gave "according to his ability" to help the Jerusalem church, even though the prophecy probably did not tell them to do this. Nonetheless, out of their desire to care for one another as a family, including those outside their cohesive group, they set aside funds to help their brethren, and sent them with Paul and Barnabas to Jerusalem.

When Paul arrived in Jerusalem with the money, he gave it to the leaders of the church and then met with the apostles (Gal 2:1-10). Their response to Paul's ministry of the gospel to the Gentiles was one of great joy, and their only instruction to him was "to continue to remember the poor." This, Paul says, was the "very thing I was eager to do" (Gal 2:10). Paul did indeed continue to "remember the poor," and he exhorted his churches to do the same. After the Antioch experience, this sharing of resources was not confined within specific churches, but extended to the larger family of God throughout the region in which the gospel had been preached. Over and over in his letters Paul exhorts his churches to take up "the collection for the saints" (see 1 Cor 16:1).

These inter-church gifts not only helped the poorer church in Judea, but made the "unity of the Spirit" between the Jewish and Gentile churches a practical reality. Although Paul often supported himself by making tents (Acts 18:1-4), he considered the monetary gift the Philippian church sent him to be "a fragrant offering, a sacrifice acceptable and pleasing to God" (Phil 4:18). But to Paul, the actual gift was secondary to the attitude which prompted it: "Not that I seek the gift; but I seek the fruit which increases to your credit" (Phil 4:17). The important thing for Paul was that believers have an attitude of watch-care for one another. This attitude would naturally result in sharing among them.

The Gentile churches to whom Paul ministered must have been somewhat better off financially than the mother church in Jerusalem. Many from the Gentile upper classes responded to the gospel (Acts 17:4, 12). This relative affluence may have limited the possibility of material sharing within the churches, forcing them to channel their desire to care for one another into inter-community giving.

As we might expect, Paul's emphasis on community and sharing in the church sometimes caused problems. There were those who used the church's omnipresent caring attitude as an excuse for laziness. The apostle condemns this attitude sharply, saying, "Even when we were with you, we gave you this command: If any one will not work, let him not eat" (2 Thes 3:10). The fact that Paul had to repeat this instruction is significant. It suggests that the church was zealous to maintain a sharing community life, even if this practice was sometimes abused. However, Paul makes it very clear that his command is intended to protect community. After exhorting the offenders to earn their own bread, he immediately cautions the rest, "Brethren, do not be weary in well-doing" (2 Thes 3:13) in case they might misunderstand his exhortation and stop sharing altogether.

The priority Paul placed on the basic attitude of watch-care among believers is borne out in his instruction on Christian freedom. He exhorts both the churches in Rome (Rom 14-15) and in

Corinth (1 Cor 8) to be careful that the liberty they have does not do harm to another. Even though Christians are free toward all things, it is valuable for liberty to be curtailed on account of a brother or sister. Again we see community not only in material things but in a basic attitude of care for one another in all spheres of life.

Paul saw that as a result of this attitude, the members of a community would be "*of the same mind* with one another according to Christ Jesus" and they would "with *one accord* (and) with *one voice* glorify the God and Father of our Lord Jesus Christ" (Rom 15:5-6). As community operates in the material, spiritual, and social areas of our lives, the "one new man" really does act as one.

The Image of God in Community

The emphasis on community in the Jerusalem church and in Paul's Gentile churches didn't happen by accident; it was the plan of the Holy Spirit from the beginning that the assembly of believers should act as a family — as "one new man." The apostles understood this unity to be part of the fundamental nature of the church and they took steps to see that community was part of the day-to-day experience of every Christian. It is clear from their letters, especially in Paul's discourses on the church, that the apostles wanted to build churches which displayed both facets of the image of God. The churches were to act vertically in worship on the basis of their restored relationship with God and horizontally in community on the basis of their restored relationships with men.

We sometimes read Paul's letters without realizing the depth of his dedication to the church as a family. For him, it is a foundational principle that because all Christians have been adopted as sons and daughters of God, they must relate to each other as brothers and sisters. Paul showed the way in this by addressing them, as "brethren." We forget the radical reorientation of thinking that this form of address must have required in him. In his former life as "a Pharisee of Pharisees," it was unthinkable for him to even come under the same roof with a Gentile "dog." Yet now he speaks of these same "dogs" in unmistakably intimate terms as "brethren" — members of his family.

In this one word "brethren" Paul packs much of the beauty of his theology of the church. This Pharisee, zealous for the Jewish faith above all his contemporaries, could consider himself a brother to Gentiles who were by birth and behavior opposed to everything for which he previously had stood. The reason, Paul makes clear, is that something revolutionary indeed happened when Jesus broke down the dividing wall between Jew and Gentile on the cross.

When Paul speaks specifically of the formation of "one new man" through the work of Christ, he insists on the centrality of this reconciliation of divided people.

> For he [Christ] is our peace, who has made us both [Jew and Gentile] one, and has broken down the dividing wall of hostility, by abolishing in his flesh the law of commandments and ordinances, that he might *create* in himself one new man in place of the two, so making peace, and might reconcile us both to God in one body through the cross, thereby bringing the hostility to an end. . . . So then you are no longer strangers and sojourners, but you are fellow citizens with the saints and members of the household of God. (Eph 2:14-16, 19)

The line of reasoning here is important. Christ himself is the peace between Jew and Gentile for he "created" the two warring groups into one new man. This work of Christ makes us part of God's household. Community never comes of its own accord but only as a result of Christ's work on the cross. A group of strict, orthodox Jews could never have gotten together with a group of rank pagans and tried to act as a family. The barrier between them — the Law — was still standing. In Christ, the barrier between them was destroyed. In the first century church, Jews and Gentiles *did* come together as one family, and, although there were some tense moments, it worked.

The community which the church experiences is not merely the endeavor of men; it is something created by God. This is "the fellowship of the Holy Spirit" (2 Cor 13:14) which is just as much the work of the Triune God as is "the grace of the Lord Jesus

Christ, and the love of God." It is nonsense to talk of the family-hood of Christians unless each member of the family is in relation to God as Father.

Our relationship with God as Father comes before community. It will not work the other direction. No matter how hard we try, community among men will not bring about communion with God. We cannot come into relationship with God as Father by working from our humanity alone to establish a community. In the end, such an effort will only bring us further into alienation from each other, never into familyhood. The foundation of community is *only* in the work of the Holy Spirit and in Christ's new creation of "one new man."

The apostles recognized that since the church was one new man—the image bearer of God—it should display both the vertical and horizontal relationships of the image. This was the uniqueness of the early church. It was the reason why the church turned the world upside down. Christians did not act as a "movement" with a common cause or program. They did not act like a club with a common interest or experience. The Christians acted like a family, meeting each other's needs any way they could. It was this essential familyhood, founded on what God has done, that formed the basis for all their actions.

Community Is Not an Option

It is easy to see in the Acts narrative that the function of the church as a family—what we have called community—was a fundamental part of the early Christians' experience. In modern times, we have said in effect that community is an optional thing, something to be taken seriously only by the lunatic fringe of the church. However, we must be honest enough to admit that this modern view is a conclusion based on our own prejudices and nowhere expressed in the New Testament. To the extent that we regard community as an option, we move away from apostolic teaching and from orthodoxy of life (ortho*praxy*), into an area that can be called heteropraxy—a life which is qualitatively different than that of the apostolic church.

The non-optional nature of community is obvious not only in

the brief glimpses of church life we have in Acts and Paul's instructions on the "collection for the saints," but comes into the foreground often in the Epistles. Since the image of God displayed in the church has a manward facet and a Godward facet, we should expect to see community among men as a constant companion of Christians' new-found communion with God. This is precisely what we do see. The New Testament letters bring us face to face with the inseparability of community with men and communion with God.

In their letters to churches, the apostles treat the importance of the dual relationships of the image of God—communion and community—in a matter-of-fact way. Paul, for instance, gives thanks concerning the Ephesian church for two reasons: their faith in the Lord, and their love for the saints. "For this reason, because I have heard of your faith in the Lord Jesus [a proper vertical relationship], *and* your love toward all the saints [proper horizontal relationships], I do not cease to give thanks for you, remembering you in my prayers" (Eph 1:15-16).

The letter to the Hebrews makes the same correlation between the vertical and horizontal relationships of the image of God. Here, the section containing exhortations about worship is followed immediately by exhortations about community. "Therefore let us be grateful for receiving a kingdom that cannot be shaken, and thus let us offer to God acceptable worship, with reverence and awe; for our God is a consuming fire. Let brotherly love continue. Do not neglect to show hospitality to strangers. . ." (Heb 12:28-13:2). The chapter division obscures this relationship, but it is clear in the original letter.

The importance of both the vertical and horizontal aspects of the image of God is stated in even more striking terms later in the same letter: "Through Jesus, therefore, let us continually offer to God a sacrifice of praise—the fruit of lips that confess his name. *And* do not forget to do good and share with others for with such sacrifices [notice the plural] God is pleased" (Heb 13:15-16). Here, both worshipping God and sharing with the brethren are the sacrifices which please God.

Statements like these occur throughout the New Testament Epistles (see James 3:9-10; Heb 6:10). But the most forceful statement of the partnership between the two aspects of the image of God occurs in the first letter of John.

John was apparently confronted with a type of Gnostic spiritualizing which regarded community relationships among believers as unimportant. The Gnostic teaching about the centrality of spiritual enlightenment (the "gnosis" or "knowledge"), and the evil nature of everything material led to an indifferent attitude toward community. John condemns this in no uncertain terms. For John, love of God and love of your brethren are inseparable; Christians cannot have one without the other.

This inseparability of the Godward and manward relationships of the image of God is a recurring theme in 1 John. For instance, he says, "He who says he is in the light and hates his brother is in the darkness still. He who loves his brother abides in the light, and in it there is no cause for stumbling" (1 Jn 2:9-10). He makes a similar, though more detailed, argument in 3:10-20 which is summarized in the statement, "We know that we have passed out of death into life, because we love the brethren. He who does not love remains in death" (3:14). John does not teach that you come into "light" or "life" — the fruit of our relationship with God — by loving the brethren. Loving the brethren will not *bring* a man into salvation, but loving the brethren is a necessary *result* of salvation.

This is why he says that the commandment of God has two parts, "And this *is* his commandment [singular], that we should believe in the name of his Son Jesus Christ *and* love one another, just as he has commanded us" (1 Jn 3:23). There is but one commandment here: To display both the vertical and horizontal facets of the image of God. John cautions us against the idea that the love which God commands is a mere abstract oneness: "Little children, let us not love in word or speech but in deed and in truth" (3:18). The love to which the beloved disciple continually exhorts us in this letter is a love that is embodied in the day-by-day life of community. It is never something that is true "in the heavenlies" but has no reality in our lives.

After repeatedly emphasizing the importance of both loving the brethren and loving God (4:7-8, 11-12, 20-21), John caps his argument. In 5:1 he tells his readers why his teaching is true:

"Everyone who believes that Jesus is the Christ is born of God; *and everyone who loves the father loves his child as well.*" By faith we become God's children, and we become brethren to one another. How can we love our Father but not his other children, our brethren? It is impossible. Indeed, it never occurred to John or anyone else in apostolic times (certainly not to Jesus; see Mt 6:12, 14; 18:23-35) that it was possible to be in communion with God without being in community with men.

However, like the Gnostics John wrote against, we have made our relationship with God into a "knowledge" that has little bearing on how we relate to one another. We have tried to divide the image of God, accepting what is comfortable and ignoring the rest. Though we may have maintained our orthodoxy, we have lost our orthopraxy.

This is the tragedy of the modern church: We are not being who we are created to be. We are created to bear God's image before the world, in both its horizontal and vertical facets. We are created to bear God's image visibly, not only in words, but in "actions and in truth." We are created to act as a family, honoring God as our Father and caring for each other as his children.

The Essence of Community

There are a great many ways this essential familyhood can be manifested. But no matter what form it takes, certain attitudes need to characterize us as a people and mold our understanding of community.

1. Community is visible.

The community which God's children enjoy is a *visible community*. The apostles would have been quite upset had anyone dared to tell them that the only community we have is in the "mystical body of Christ." Of course it is true that we have a grand community with all believers from all places and all times in the heavenlies. But if that is the *only* community we have, we are an impoverished people. The great family of God in the heavenlies has its fallen, finite, but redeemed counterpart on earth.

We are called to love one another "in deed and truth" on earth as well as in heaven, caring for one another in our day-to-day lives in a damaged world. Our community will be imperfect because we are imperfect. But if we are serious about the work of God conforming us to the image of his son (Rom 8:29), we must look for a substantial renewal of our relationships as brethren, children of one Father, just as we have substantial renewal of our individual relationships with the Father.

2. Community is total.

Community in the Christian sense is a *total community*; it involves whole people ministering to one another as whole people. The church is not only a place for what we could call "spiritual" ministry, although it certainly must include that. It is also to be a place where the saints of God care for one another in all areas of their lives: including the spiritual, social, psychological, and material.

In Acts, the brethren of the Jerusalem church did not limit themselves to a specific area of ministry, such as praying for one another. They devoted themselves to the apostles' teaching and prayer, took many of their meals together, had fellowship, shared their property in order to meet physical needs, and did a host of other things. They did not care for each other's spiritual needs only. They cared for each other's needs no matter what they were. This is Christian community in its fullest sense.

3. Community is a daily event.

The church is the family of God *daily*, not one day a week. We cannot have community in the New Testament sense if we see each other on Sunday morning and live in isolation the next six days. In Jerusalem, "all who believed were together" (Acts 2:44). They did not have one big meeting that lasted all week, but they were involved in each other's lives on a day-to-day basis, eating together, praying together, and simply enjoying one another's company. This type of daily ministry to each other is essential if we are to act as a family.

Of course this does not mean that "community" is a thing to be added to our list of daily responsibilities. The New Testament does not intend that the necessity of community among Christians become some kind of new Law like "Thou shalt not have a day without community." There are times when solitude is a good thing for a Christian. The point is that community must be a frequent part of our lives, not an occasional part. A friend of mine has a poster which reads, "Seven days without prayer makes one weak." We could say the same thing about community, because from the biblical perspective, community is like food. Christians not only have to eat it to stay alive, but they want to eat it because God made it taste so good!

4. *Community is catholic.*

The family of God is not composed only of those within our own cohesive group, but extends around the world. It is a *catholic community.* We must understand that the catholic (universal) church is in a sense one community. The church at Antioch shared willingly with the church at Jerusalem because it recognized that both churches belonged to the same family.

A narrow-minded, sectarian view of the Body of Christ will never bring us anything but the worst kind of parochialism. We need to recognize the whole church as one family, not necessarily under one giant administrative umbrella, but nonethcless *one.* We need to be willing to minister to one another outside our own cohesive group or denominational structure.

The Practice of Community

How can the church go about living its true nature as a visible, total, daily, and catholic community? I hesitate to give a prescription, because every expression of community is (or should be) unique and should apply the biblical attitude of watch-care in its own way. I will, however, give a few examples of ways in which churches have sought to be communities, in order to illustrate the wide-ranging freedom within the biblical norm of the fellowship of the Holy Spirit.

One option for a large church (fifty or more active members) is to break up the church into smaller (ten to twenty person) groups. These groups could be viewed as "house churches" within the larger church and could devote themselves to Bible study and ministry to one another. Such small groups could be organized geographically, by age group, or by common interest, so that people would be better able to take an active part in each other's lives outside the meetings of the group.

This is not to say that each small group would necessarily be a self-sufficient church. The larger church would continue to have its ongoing identity in worship, teaching, mission, and so on. But it would have a number of smaller identities within it, just as many churches do now with mid-week Bible studies, prayer meetings, and young people's groups. The difference would be that the "house church" groups would exist specifically to encourage community and would engage in various activities as parts of that purpose. By contrast, most "church groups" exist for some specific goal, such as prayer, and encourage community only as a byproduct of that specific goal.

Another option would be for people in a church to move close together, deliberately forming several geographic "communities" in which they could share each other's lives on a day-to-day basis. The larger church would then be comprised of a number of small collections of Christians living within a few blocks of each other. Obviously, this pattern is far better suited to a city church than to a rural one.

Finally, it is possible to practice community across the boundaries of existing churches. A neighborhood or office Bible study of Christians who are members of various churches might well evolve into a setting where people's needs for caring and community can be met. Groups like these need not be divisive (although this possibility does exist). They can be places of support and ministry for helping their members to be better able to function in their own churches.

In our church, for instance, we utilize a combination of forms to help us care for one another as a community. Many of us live in a defined geographical community of about twenty square blocks. Although in the beginning, some of us were skeptical about the value of living close together, it has proven to be very helpful. It is no longer difficult to visit someone else in the church; they live nearby. Even in our cold New England winters, it is no great bother to walk a block or two to pray with someone on short notice, or to have dinner together.

A geographical community is especially valuable to us because we live in a densely populated urban area. It would be less advantageous in a suburban or rural setting. But even in our urban situation, there are a number of people in the church who do not live within walking distance of others. So to be sure that each person's need for community is met, each person in the church belongs to a small group—a kind of "house church."

These small groups all started out with the same goals and format, but they are now quite different because they have developed according to the needs of the members of the groups. One group is engaged in in-depth Bible study, another in learning to worship more fully, another in praying for each other. Despite these differences, the members of all the groups are seeking to meet each other's physical, social, emotional, and spiritual needs. Their goal is to be built together in intimate relationships.

Of course, this is just one way of seeking community. It happens to work in our particular situation. There are probably dozens of other ways for the church to act out its nature as one new man. The issue is not the specific form which community takes. The issue is that visible, total, daily, catholic community is not an optional part of Christianity. Community is at the core of what it means for the church and individual Christians to be bearers of the image of God. If we treat community as inconsequential, we are being unbiblical in our approach to the Christian life. We are also giving the world a warped view of the image of God.

FIVE

YOUR SPIRITUAL SERVICE
OF WORSHIP

IN a sense, the discussion in the last chapter has made an artificial division between the horizontal and vertical facets of the image of God. It has been convenient for us to consider the New Testament concept of community by itself. However, we must constantly remind ourselves that community, for all its importance, is not sufficient in itself. God's image is twofold: manward and Godward. To exalt community as the single goal of Christ's church is a dangerous half-truth. God desires to have a community, a kingdom, but one with a special nature. It is to be a kingdom of priests (Rv 1:6). We dare not raise the familyhood of Christians to a place above the Fatherhood of God over them. If we do, we will lose both, for we are called together as a community because of our relationship with him.

As image bearers of God, we are called not only to be his family but also to be his worshippers. When we become Christians, our relationship with God is re-created. We are transformed from rebels living in alienation from him into children living in his household (Eph 2:1-3, 19). This radical change renews us to the roots of our beings. Previously, we had a negative relationship with God; now we have been brought to a positive relationship with him not merely as slaves, or even as friends, but as his own children.

Because we are God's children, we can dare to speak to him intimately as "Father." Yet at the same time we must be conscious of him as our Creator and our God. He is the Creator; we are creatures. Our intimacy with him as Father needs to be coupled with our awe of him as the one who builds all things—from trees to galaxies. Our attitude toward him should be neither an adolescent friendliness nor the abject fear of slaves before their master. Our relationship with God is to transcend both of these, for the awesome Lord of the universe is at the same time our own Father.

Our proper attitude toward God can be described as one of worshipful intimacy. Jesus taught his disciples this balance in the Lord's Prayer. He told the disciples to address God intimately as "Our Father in heaven," but to follow that with "hallowed be your name," emphasizing God's greatness and power. This attitude of worshipful intimacy allows us to take up our proper position before God not only as his beloved children but as his worshipping creatures.

God is not neutral about receiving worship from his creatures. Even the inanimate creation is to give God praise. The psalm says it this way:

Praise him, sun and moon,
    praise him, all you shining stars!
Praise him, you highest heavens,
    and you waters above heavens!
Let them praise the name of the Lord!
    For he commanded and they were created. (Ps 148:3-5)

God is to be worshipped by the whole creation, even by the sun and moon and stars. Through the vast reaches of the universe, they declare his majesty and glory (Rom 1:20).

The Importance of Worship

God desires worship from human beings as well. We are called to give God praise not only as the rest of creation gives it, but in a much more precise way because we bear his image. Jesus said that we are to worship "in spirit and in truth," and he said that God not only desires but even *seeks* such worshippers (Jn 4:23). Worshipping God, like community, is not an optional part of the

Christian life; it lies at the very core of Christianity. Worship is something God seeks. Our entire life is to be characterized by praise and thanksgiving, which are the proper content of worship (Ps 50:7-14, 23). In fact, Paul flatly says that it is God's will for us to offer thanksgiving to him and so be his worshippers (1 Thes 5:18).

Our call to be worshipping children of God means that we should set aside special times each day to thank God for his goodness to us. However, these special times do not exhaust our role as the worshippers of God. When God blesses us, we need to thank him. Even when something bad or inconvenient happens, we need to praise him because "in *all* things God works for the good of those who love him" (Rom 8:28).

Yet our worship of God as his image bearers has a corporate aspect as well. God has also called the church, as his image bearer, to worship him as a community. Paul tells the people of the church at Rome to "present your bodies [plural] as a living sacrifice [singular],...which *is* your spiritual worship" (Rom 12:1). In corporate worship something unique happens so that *many* human beings can present themselves to God as *one* living sacrifice.

Corporate worship has always characterized the life of the church. The early church saw its worship to be central to its existence. Its persecutors understood this, and became convinced that if they could disrupt the church's worship, they could destroy the church. Thus the Christians kept their pre-dawn worship meetings secret. Yet they attached such great importance to these meetings that non-attendance was unthinkable unless a person was too ill to come.

In order to understand the importance of worship as a community, we need to recall once again that the church is not simply a collection of individual believers, but also "one new man" having a sense of corporate identity. Thus the worship of the church is not merely the sum of the worship of the individuals present. The church itself worships as one being, as the one new man which bears God's image.

As we will see later, part of the reason why Paul was concerned over the church at Corinth was that its members behaved only as a collection of individuals when they met for worship. Each person was acting independently of the others. They were not lacking in any spiritual gift; they were lacking in their appreciation of the worship of the church as the worship of "one new man." They had no sense of the interdependence that presents many bodies as one "living and holy sacrifice."

We have already seen something of this interdependence in Paul's metaphor of the church as "the body of Christ." The members of the body are different and each depends on the others so that the whole body might function. This metaphor has a direct application to the church's worship. In fact, it occurs in its most elaborate form (1 Cor 12:12-27) in the midst of the longest New Testament passage on corporate worship (1 Cor 11-14). However, Paul and other apostolic writers use another picture to focus their teaching about the corporate nature of the church's worship. This is the picture of the "one new man" as the temple of the living God.

The New Man as a Temple

In Ephesians 2, Paul conceptualizes the church as the temple of the living God. His line of reasoning begins in verse 11 where he speaks of the Gentiles who had previously lived in a state of alienation from God and from his people Israel (vv. 11-12). In Christ, however, the two warring groups, Jew and Gentile, were brought to peace and formed by Christ into "one new man." The two groups together ("in one body") are reconciled to God. In this action, God made one way of salvation available to both the Gentile ("those who were far away") and to the Jew ("those who were near"), and gave them one way of access to himself, Christ Jesus (vv. 17-18). God's work in creating this new man is the basis for the community which God's people have.

Then, in verse 19, Paul makes a transition from the concept of the church as God's household to the church as God's house.

So then you [Gentiles] are no longer strangers and sojourners, but you are fellow citizens with the saints and *members of the household of God*, built upon the foundation of the apostles and prophets, Christ Jesus himself being the chief cornerstone, in whom the whole *structure* is joined together and *grows into a holy temple* in the Lord; in whom you also are built into it for *a dwelling place of God* in the Spirit. (Eph 2:19-22)

The one new man brings Jew and Gentile together as members of God's own family, the church. But now Paul develops his thought further: Not only are we of God's household (his family), but we have also been *"built upon the foundations* of the apostles and prophets." We are called a "building," and a "dwelling place of God." In short, we are God's *house* as well as his household.

This metaphor is not just an idle play on words, but is central to Paul's teaching in Ephesians. The "one new man" is not only God's *family* because of Christ's work, but is also God's *dwelling place.* The picture Paul has in mind here is that of the temple in Jerusalem. When Solomon dedicated the first temple, he said, "I have built Thee an exalted house and a place for Thy dwelling forever" (2 Chr 6:2). Although Solomon knew that the Creator of the universe was far too "big" to dwell in a building (2 Chr 6:18), there was a sense in which God really lived in his temple (2 Chr 7:16): He was present there in a special way.

The thought in Ephesians 2:20-22 is that the church is part of the reality which the temple in Jerusalem foreshadowed. The true temple is built on the foundation of the apostles and prophets, and the cornerstone is Christ himself—the ultimate revelation of God (Heb 1:1-2). Christ holds the building together; it is "in him" that it "grows into" [another good translation would be "rises to become"] a holy temple. The temple in Jerusalem was inorganic, made of stones and wood. But the one new man is organic—it is made up of human beings and "grows into" a temple. Both temples are alike, though, because God dwells in the church in a unique sense, just as, under the Old Covenant, God dwelt in the Jerusalem temple.

The fact that God dwells in the one new man, the church, is by no means to be opposed to the fact that God dwells in each believer. In 1 Corinthians 6:19, arguing against immoral behavior, Paul says, "Do you not know that your body is a *temple* of the

Holy Spirit within you, which you have from God?" The Christian's sexual ethic is based on the understanding that God the Holy Spirit dwells in every believer (Rom 8:9). Paul uses the same word "temple" to describe the individual that he used in Ephesians 2:21 to describe the church. We must not choose between the individual and the church as the temple of God. The calling of every believer is to be an appropriate dwelling place of God; this is the calling of the church as well as the individual.

Earlier in 1 Corinthians, Paul pictures the church, not the individual, as the temple. In 1 Corinthians 3, he speaks of his apostolic work, first condemning the Corinthians' partisan spirit (vv. 1-5) and then saying that all workers are farming the same field (vv. 6-9) and building the same building (vv. 9-15). Then, in terms almost identical to those he uses in his later exhortation to individuals in 1 Corinthians 6:19, he says to the church, "Do you not know that you are God's temple and that God's Spirit dwells in you?" (1 Cor 3:16). The church is many people acting as *one* temple. Paul even introduces his exhortation by calling the church "God's building" (1 Cor 3:9). Paul had enough fluidity of thought to describe both the individual and the church as "a temple." We should do the same.

The concept of the church as a temple is not peculiar to Paul, but figures in the thoughts of other New Testament writers as well (1 Pt 2:4-5; Heb 3:1-6). The letter to the Hebrews, though, uses the church-temple illustration not for its own sake, but to support another point—the superiority of Christ. The burden of Hebrews is to show that Christ and his New Covenant transcend everyone and everything that had come from God previously. In Hebrews 3, the point is specifically that Christ is superior to Moses.

> He [Jesus] was faithful to him who appointed him, just as Moses was faithful in *God's house*. Yet Jesus has been counted worthy of as much more glory than Moses as the builder of a house has more honor than the house. (For every house is built by someone, but the builder of all things is God). Now Moses was faithful in all *God's house* as a servant, to testify to the things that were to be spoken later, but Christ was faithful over *God's house* as a son. *And we are his house.* (Heb 3:2-6)

Here, the typology of the church as the temple of God is explicitly carried out. Moses was faithful as a servant in God's house, but Christ is faithful as a son over God's house; in fact, *we are* his house. In this instance, as we have seen in Paul's letters, God dwells in one house made up of many people. Christ built the house and rules over it as God's son. By contrast, Moses was part of God's house. Therefore, Christ deserves much more glory than Moses, just as the builder of a house deserves more glory than the house he built. God's people, including Moses, are God's house. The church, as the house of God, is the present reality toward which the Old Testament temple pointed.

Israel's temple was primarily the place where God was to be worshipped. Yet the temple, and the mobile tabernacle which came before it, served many other functions in Old Testament times. It was the forum for the political life of the people, for Israel was a theocracy where God was truly to reign as King. The annual festivals all centered around the temple, making it important to Israel's social life as well. But above all, it was the center of worship. Before the dispersion of the Jews and the rise of the synagogue, it was inconceivable that God could be rightly worshipped anywhere except at the temple. In a very special way, he dwelt there — it was *his house.* Indeed, Jeroboam's sin after the civil war between Judah and Israel was not only teaching the people to worship images but also teaching them to worship at a place other than the Jerusalem temple (1 Kgs 12:25-33).

In the same way, the temple of the church has its primary function as the center of worship. The church also relates to many other spheres of life — such as the political, social, and spiritual — just as the Jerusalem temple focused the many spheres of Israel's life. However, when the New Testament writers refer to the church as God's temple, they are primarily interested in seeing it as a worshipping community.

For example, Peter says, "Like living stones be yourselves built into a spiritual house [a temple], to be a holy priesthood, to offer spiritual sacrifices acceptable to God through Jesus Christ" (1 Pt 2:5). The spiritual house made up of living stones is to be a place where God's people exercise their priestly role. Note that here, as in Ephesians 2, we *are* the house and we are those (priests) who are *in* the house. The house we *are* provides the environment for our worship *in* the house.

The uniqueness of corporate worship becomes obvious in Peter's teaching that we are "living stones being built into a spiritual house." One stone is not a temple. Many stones must be built together before a temple exists. Similarly, one stone, one Christian, can indeed worship God and minister to him, but the temple of believers is not formed until they finally meet together for worship as a community. The church is a temple made "without hands," a fitting dwelling place for God. In fact, it is the place where God will dwell for all eternity (Rv 21:2-3).

The "Building Up" of the New Temple

One important difference between the inanimate temple of the Old Covenant and the organic temple of the New, is the fact that the new temple is "being built up." Both Peter and Paul speak of *"being built* into a spiritual house" (1 Pt 2:5; Eph 2:20-22). By contrast, Israel's temple was a static structure. In Jerusalem, it was a structure that stood in one place. During the wilderness journey, the tabernacle was pre-fabricated. But it was still a static structure which people set up wherever they camped.

Both Ephesians 2 and 1 Peter 2 make clear that the church is in no sense a static structure. It is "being built up," being "joined together," "growing," "being built together" into a temple. The church is truly organic; it is not a building you come *to*, but a building you come *to be*. It is not an edifice on a street corner, but a structure of living stones, made anew each time it comes together.

This concept of the "building up" of the church as a temple is fundamental to an understanding of the uniqueness of corporate worship. The church should never worship as a pile of living stones strewn all over the landscape. Rather, we are to worship as a temple where living stones are put together into a building, each stone precisely shaped to fit in a certain place in the temple.

The loss of this concept of being "built together" is one of the major deficiencies in our modern idea of Christian worship. The idea of being "built together" implies some kind of commonality.

Without a measure of common life as a community, a building-together of the temple may be a heavenly reality, but not an earthly one. How can people be built together *practically* if they see each other for an hour every Sunday morning, and have very little contact with each other even during that time? Our modern forms of worship may be adequate for some important functions of the church such as preaching from the scriptures, but it leaves something to be desired as a format for the worship of God.

When we use such a format for worship, our worship usually remains essentially individualistic. Although we are together, we might as well each be put in a plexiglass cubicle, isolated from everyone else. We might learn something from the sermon, or enjoy the sound of the singing. But much the same thing would happen if we were to stay at home and listen to a taped message and choir, for no true "building together" has occurred. We have worshipped as a jumbled pile of living stones, not as a temple.

The church at Corinth had exactly this problem when it worshipped. The members' attitudes toward the Lord's Supper and the function of spiritual gifts were results of an individualistic view of corporate worship. When they ate the Lord's Supper together, each one treated it as if it were his own meal. One person would drink far too much of the wine, ending up drunk. Another would eat most of the bread so that some members were entirely left out (1 Cor 11:20-21).

Paul's outrage at this is evident. He tells them that they are not really eating the Lord's Supper at all, but each is eating it as if it were his alone. Imagine someone coming into your church during the sacrament and shouting, "This is not the Lord's Supper! You're not eating it together—each one is pretending that he is alone, even in this crowd!" That would be quite a shock, but that is essentially what Paul did. He even told the Corinthians that their meetings "do more harm than good" (v. 17) and that they "despise the church of God" (v. 22).

These are strong words. Paul is so harsh because the Corinthians are not "recognizing the body of the Lord" (v. 29). In context, this seems to refer not to the bread of the communion but to the body of Christ—the church. They had not recognized the body of Christ; they had not acted according to the corporate nature of the church in worship. Instead they had acted out of selfish individualism and had ignored their calling to worship God as one new man. Paul closes his exhortation with, "So then, my brethren, when you come together to eat, wait for one another" (v. 33). The Lord's Supper is a truly corporate event, not to be engaged in as an unconnected pile of "living stones," but as a "built-together" temple.

The Corinthians betrayed the same individualistic attitude toward the use of spiritual gifts. Paul begins his discussion with, "Now concerning spiritual gifts, brethren, I do not want you to be uninformed" (12:1), but he tells them very little about the *nature* of the spiritual gifts. Instead, he tells them a great deal about the *use* of the spiritual gifts. His point is that the church is one amidst the diversity of spiritual gifts. The Corinthians' mistake was not that they were using the more exotic spiritual gifts (which Paul nowhere condemns), but that they were using them in an individualistic manner, without regard for the building up of the church (14:12).

The apostle applies the "body of Christ" metaphor directly to this point. The reason God has given a diversity of spiritual gifts to the church is "that there may be no discord in the body" (12:25). Each member of the body is needed (12:15-16) and needs the contributions of the other members (12:17). The life of the church as a body is dependent on the members' need for one another. They should no longer use their gifts individualistically; they are to use them to build up the one new man.

In 1 Corinthians 13, Paul shows them "a still more excellent way" (12:31) — that is, the way of love. Love is "a still more excellent way" of doing what? The answer lies back in verse 25: "that there may be no discord in the body." Love, in this passage, is not the most excellent way to spirituality but the most excellent way to unify the body of Christ. Spiritual gifts help unify the body, but, if they are to aid unity, they must be used in love.

Thus Paul's famous chapter on love (1 Cor 13) refers to the proper use of spiritual gifts: They must be used in an attitude of love toward the rest of the church or they are worth absolutely nothing (13:1-3). If we use spiritual gifts individualistically, to elevate ourselves, they will fragment the body instead of building it up. However, when the gifts are exercised in love, they will bring beauty and oneness into the expression of the body-hood of the body of Christ.

Spiritual Gifts

To stress the connection between his teaching on the body (chapter 12) and his teaching on love (chapter 13), Paul combines them and makes them uncomfortably practical in chapter 14. He chooses tongues and prophecy as examples for instruction about the proper exercise of spiritual gifts. He repeats that the gifts are to be used for "edification" (vv. 3, 4, 5, 12, 17, and 26). The Greek word Paul uses which is translated "edification" is the same word translated "building up" in Ephesians 2 and 1 Peter 2. Proper use of the spiritual gifts will "build up" the church as a temple.

"Edification" in 1 Corinthians 14 is not a description of a good feeling one has. Edification is the process by which the individual living stones are put together into a temple. People often say things like, "That was an edifying message tonight," meaning that the sermon made them feel good. This may be a legitimate use of the word, but it is not Paul's use here. He uses "edify" in the sense of building an edifice. Edification is the process of placing one living stone on top of another to build the building of God's church.

Spiritual gifts exercised in love will edify the church in this sense. They will build it up. They are one of the ways that a collection of stones is built into a dwelling place for God. Thus Paul says, "When you come together, everyone has a hymn, or a word of instruction, a revelation, a tongue, or an interpretation. All of these must be done for the strengthening ["building up," "edification"] of the church" (1 Cor 14:26).

The edification or building up of the church is a very important aspect of Paul's vision for worship as a community. Corporate worship must not be merely a collection of individuals worshipping at the same place. In worship, the church must act as *one* new man—the organic temple of God. The Corinthians had a mere collectivism in worship—they got together in one place and worshipped individualistically. Paul wanted them to be a unity of diverse living stones that could act like they were "the body of Christ and individually members of it" (1 Cor 12:27).

It is important to realize that, because each stone in the organic temple is fitted for a particular place in the building, each is unique. Every member is different. Too often, we end up with uniformity when we strive for unity in the church. We tend to want all the stones in the temple to be the same size and shape, never considering that God wants some to be ceiling tiles and some support beams and some filigreed pillars and some foundation stones. God has not made us all the same; he has made each of us unique and important.

Paul's exhortation that in worship "everyone has a hymn or a word of instruction, a revelation, a tongue, or an interpretation" is fundamental to understanding corporate worship. Each individual believer has a unique part to play in worship. However, the individual's contribution is not individualistic but rather for the building of the corporate temple.

The same concept underlies Paul's teaching about the use of spiritual gifts. Not everyone has the same gift (1 Cor 12:29-31), and even similar gifts are exercised in different ways. God has ordained this so that no one person can see himself individualistically, but must be dependent on other members' gifts (12:21-25). God has designed the church so that it has a diversity of gifts within the unity of the one new man. The church is to be one unified body held together by a diversity of individuals working together in love.

Indeed this unity in diversity was foreshadowed in the temple of the Old Covenant. 2 Chronicles 3-4 describes the diverse beauty of the temple: Cypress beams, gold leaf walls, linen hangings of purple and crimson, sculptured angels, and all kinds of rare gems. And Solomon's temple is a mere *shadow* of the New Testament temple!

God did not expect his temple to be a bland,.gray structure; neither does he expect the church to be characterized by a drab uniformity! It is the diversity of the church which makes it such a spectacular part of the new creation, for it is only by being a unity of diverse members that the one new man can be truly bodylike and not just collective.

To consider just one example, imagine where the church would be without teachers. Not everyone in the church is gifted to communicate the truths of scripture; so those who do not have such gifts are forced to rely on those who do. The problem comes when this is the only gift being expressed in the church. The rest of the body relies on those who are teachers, but on whom do the teachers rely? If the only gifts we recognize are those of teachers, we turn the church into a mouth instead of a body. How grotesque it would be to look up and see a mouth walking down the street when you expected to see a whole body! Yet this is what we try to do to the body of Christ when we see it only in terms of a few specialized gifts.

The body of Christ is not a place where everyone in the church is dependent on one person — the pastor, teacher, or evangelist. Instead there is to be an *inter*dependence of each member on all the others. God has gifted *each* member of the church uniquely. God has given *each* person an important function; without each function, the church is incomplete. God has designed the church so that we need one another.

This interdependence of the members of the church is the key to the function of the church as one new man in worship. When *all* the gifted people of God function in their unique roles in the church, then is the church truly built up into an organic temple which worships God.

The one new man is the organic temple of God in worship. This one new man — the church — bears the image of God because in our corporate identity we display the horizontal and vertical relationships which comprise that image.

An important question remains before us: What is unique about our worship of God as a community? Specifically, how does the corporate worship of the church uniquely bear the Godward dimension of the image of God? To answer this question, we need to examine the form of worship which has marked Christianity throughout its history.

The Image of God in Worship

There is a great diversity in the forms of modern Christian worship. Some churches are quite liturgically oriented, some have an unstructured and spontaneous worship, and many fall between these two extremes. Much of this great variety is due to the freedom given us in the New Testament. Since there is no "apostolic" form of worship laid down in the Bible, we can assume that there is nothing absolute or binding about any particular form we might choose.

Nevertheless, throughout the church's history and among the many congregations today, certain things inevitably take place in worship. These practices include prayer, scripture reading, and preaching. Most of these elements were also common to the Jewish synagogue meetings from which the early church took many of her worship forms.

However, one event made early Christian worship radically different from synagogue worship. This is the celebration of the Lord's Supper. From the first church in Jerusalem and down through the ages, the Lord's Supper has been seen as the climax of Christian worship. There has been much disagreement and division over its nature and meaning; fortunately for our purposes we need not focus on such issues. All we need to do is to recognize that the Lord's Supper was an integral part—in fact, the culmination—of early Christian worship and of Christian worship through the centuries.

As an example, let's look at the way Justin Martyr, one of the church's first apologists (around 150 A.D.), describes a meeting of his church:

And on the day called Sunday, all who live in cities or in the country gather together to one place, and the memoirs of the apostles [the New Testament] and the writings of the prophets [the Old Testament] are read, as long as time permits, then after the reader has ceased, the president (the chief elder) verbally instructs and exhorts to the imitation of these good things. Then we all rise together and pray, and, as we before said, when our prayer is ended, *bread and wine [mixed with] water* are brought, and the president in like manner offers *prayers and thanksgivings*, according to his ability, and the people assent, saying "Amen"; and there is a distribution to each, and a participation of that over which *thanks* have just been given.

(The First Apology of Justin, LXVII)

Justin wanted to give a fair description of early Christian worship in order to stop rumors that orgies and cannibalistic rites were part of the church's weekly celebration. Their pagan neighbors thought that the Christian talk of their love for one another meant that their meetings were grand orgies. They also thought that the Christians were cannibals when they partook of the body and blood of Christ. To try to stop these false rumors, Justin proposed to publish what actually went on in the Christian worship meetings. Thus his account is probably representative of Christian worship of his time, and clearly shows the climactic position of the Lord's Supper in their meetings.

Overall, the attitude that characterized these early morning meetings was one of thanksgiving. Worship was a joyful time, not an occasion for grief or sorrow. This joyful spirit of thanksgiving was so dominant that the meeting soon came to be called "eucharist," from the Greek word for "thanksgiving." The Supper—the climax of the meeting—was also called by that name: the Eucharist. This connection between worship and thanksgiving, and especially between the Lord's Supper and thanksgiving, comes through clearly in the earliest records we have of the postapostolic Christian faith.

The early church also made the connection between the Lord's Supper and thanksgiving because they saw in it a clear parallel with the Old Testament "thank offering." This sacrifice is described in Leviticus with customary attention to detail.

> If he offers it [his sacrifice] for a thanksgiving, then he shall offer with the thank offering unleavened cakes mixed with oil... And of such he shall offer one cake from each offering, as *an offering to the Lord; it shall belong to the priest* who throws the blood of the peace offerings. And the flesh of the sacrifice of his peace offerings for thanksgiving *shall be eaten on the day of his offering.* (Lv 7:12-15)

This seemingly complex ordinance worked out practically in an interesting way. After the priest offered the sacrifice to the Lord, he would take his portion, and he and the sacrificer would eat the thanksgiving offering before the Lord in a "meal before God."

The most dramatic example of this "meal before God" occurs in Exodus 24. After receiving the covenant from the Lord, Moses and the elders of Israel were told to go up to Mount Sinai to worship him (Ex 24:1-2). Accordingly, they sacrificed thank offerings (v. 5), and took the prescribed offerings with them to the mountain.

> Then Moses and Aaron, Nadab, and Abihu, and seventy of the elders of Israel went up, and *they saw the God of Israel*; and there was under his feet as it were a pavement of sapphire stone, like the very heaven for clearness. And he did not lay his hand on the chief men of the people of Israel; *they beheld God, and ate and drank.* (Ex 24:9-11)

Imagine what an experience that must have been for these seventy-some persons, sitting down to a meal before the Lord of Hosts! Yet this is what took place symbolically in every thank offering. And this is the parallel the first Christians saw between the thank offering and the Lord's Supper: Both involve a feast before the Lord.

Jesus instituted the Supper as a thing to be done "in remembrance" of him (Lk 22:19). By this he meant much more than something which brought back fond memories of events now long past. The New Covenant in Christ's blood involves not only a past event which brought the forgiveness of our sins (Heb 8:12), but also a day-to-day life as God's people in which we know him and learn from him (Heb 8:10-11).

As a result, when Christ's church celebrates communion, she is not only reminding herself of what happened the night before Jesus died, but is also re-enacting that event of intimate table fellowship the disciples shared with their Lord. The Lord's Supper is not intended to re-enact the crucifixion. It is to provide us with a continual "remembrance" of Christ's sacrifice as we, in effect, put ourselves in the place of the Twelve and dine with our Lord as Israel did in the thank offering.

When we have the Lord's Supper in our church, we often sing a song which dramatically brings out the idea of the Eucharist as a meal before God:

O welcome all you noble saints of old,
As now before your very eyes unfold
The wonders all so long ago foretold.
God and man at table are sat down.

Who is this who spreads the vict'ry feast?
Who is this who makes our warring cease?
Jesus, Risen Savior, Prince of Peace.
God and man at table are sat down.

Worship in the presence of the Lord,
With joyful songs and hearts in one accord,
And let our Host at table be adored.
God and man at table are sat down.

This song clearly expresses the fact that the Lord's Supper is a thank offering. It is a time when we can, based on the finished work of Christ, sit before God and have table fellowship with him.

In addition to "remembering," there is another element of the Lord's Supper which is found in all four New Testament records of its institution. The Lord's Supper not only *looks backward* to that last night before Jesus' crucifixion. It also *looks forward* to the fulfillment of the kingdom of God and the marriage feast we will have with the Lord Jesus when he comes again.

After Jesus had instructed the disciples to celebrate the Supper "in remembrance" of him (looking backward), the Synoptic Gospels all record him to have said something like, "For I tell you I shall not eat it until it is fulfilled in the kingdom of God" (Lk 22:16). Such remarks clearly look forward to the meal he will prepare for all Christians when he returns.

Paul's account also has this same forward and backward look to it. "For as often as you eat this bread and drink the cup, you proclaim the Lord's death [looking backward] until he comes [looking forward]" (1 Cor 11:26). Here again, the Supper looks back into history to the last Passover and the Lord's death, and also into the future to the first banquet of the fulfilled kingdom when he returns. In a real sense, it is a meal with the Lord for the time between these two meals with the Lord.

Here lies the uniqueness of the Lord's Supper and of the worship of the church as one new man: In some special sense, the Lord himself is present when his church partakes of his meal. Many theological battles have been fought over just how he is present, but for us precise definitions are not the issue. The point is that *he is there.* The parallel with the Old Testament thank offering is remarkable for, in the Lord's Supper, the Christian community dines at Christ's table. When the one new man worships, the vertical relationship with God is demonstrated as something very special. It is there that we enjoy intimate dinner table fellowship with our host, the Lord Jesus.

In human experience, the dinner table is the scene of many things, including family squabbles. But at its best, the table is the epitome of the joys of family life. It is to this joyous family intimacy of table fellowship that the church comes in the Eucharist.

Table Fellowship with God

In our table fellowship with God, the image of God is uniquely displayed by the one new man—the church. In worship, the vertical relationship of the church with God centers around this fellowship. At his table, we honor our host as our Creator and our Redeemer, acting out the intimate family relationship we have with him. When this happens in corporate worship, the church is acting both as God's household and as his house. We are his household in that we sit at his table as his family. We are his house in that he is present among us in a unique way.

The uniqueness of God's presence in corporate worship sets it apart from individual worship. When we bear God's image in worship as a community, we act as his temple and God dwells with us in a way which he doesn't in individual worship. Jesus said, "For where two or three are gathered in my name, there am I in the midst of them" (Mt 18:20). Our Lord was in no way denying his presence with us as individuals (for we are each the temple of God). Yet clearly he is present with us in a different way as we gather in his name as his church.

We need to note here that the corporate experience of the

presence of God is not some sort of new mysticism. On the contrary, this experience of one new man coming before God marks Christian worship as profoundly non-mystical. Mystical experience is essentially individual. By contrast, corporate worship is not a collection of individuals worshipping individually, but a body worshipping as a unity. Each member exercises his own function, but the outcome is not many worships; it is one worship, the worship of the whole community. This experience of many members engaging in one worship, the content of which can be communicated among them, is precisely the opposite of mystical experience.

Eastern religions, for example, lack a truly corporate concept of worship because their experience in worship is mystical by design. Although many believers in Eastern religions may gather together at one time and place, in the final analysis their worship still consists of many individual worship experiences, not one. The Eastern mystical experience, by its very nature, cannot be directly communicated, much less shared by a number of individuals simultaneously. When worship is reduced to mysticism, it cannot be truly corporate because mysticism has no directly transferable content, and must remain individualistic.

By contrast, in Christian worship, not only is communication of content possible, but this content is shared corporately by the whole church. We must never worship God merely as a collection of mystics; if we do, the corporate side of the image of God is forgotten. We are to enter into corporate worship as one new man displaying the image of God in objective, though spiritual, table fellowship with him. We worship not by seeking a mystical oneness with God, but by seeking to enter into fellowship with him as his family, displaying the image of God to the world.

One of our greatest opportunities to minister his truth into the world around us lies precisely here, in the life of the church as God's image bearer. Like the Sadducees to whom Jesus spoke, our world does not know "the Scriptures or the power of God" (Mt 22:29). We must speak, proclaiming the gospel according to the scriptures. And we must bear the image of God, demonstrating the power by which he created one new man—a worshipping community reconciled to each other and to himself. When we bear God's image toward the world, we demonstrate his power to the world. The church of God is an ongoing miracle, for he took those of us who were his enemies and made us his worshipping children.

The miracle of the church, the worshipping community, is concrete evidence that the Father sent the Son to be the Savior of the world. It demonstrates the power of God which must accompany the proclamation of the scripture to a world in search of empirical evidence for the validity of the gospel.

As we bear the image of God corporately, the world will be able to see that we are in fact a people reconciled to God and to each other. The reconciliation we have with each other is seen in our lives as a community of saints. The reconciliation we have as people with God is seen in our worship. It gives the world truth which words alone cannot provide.

Corporate worship is one of the fundamental ways for us to carry our ministry of reconciliation to the world. When the church begins to approximate its true nature as a worshipping community, it will shine forth the image of a loving, sovereign God like a city on a hill or a light in a dark place. The church as a worshipping community is another world — a different sphere of life — for there is true meaning for man in the church. In the worshipping community, man has meaning as a creature worshipping his Creator-Father, and as a member of a loving fellowship of supportive brothers and sisters. As we bear God's image in this context, we demonstrate to those around us that the words of the scriptures are true: "God *was* in Christ reconciling the world to himself" (2 Cor 5:19).

Epilogue:

The Image and Glory of God

THE IMAGE AND GLORY
OF GOD

W E who are Christians have both the privilege and the responsibility of displaying the image of God to the world around us. We are the initial manifestation of a new creation destined to include the entire created order. Thus we need to be zealous to live out our reconciliation with God and other men in both the corporate and individual spheres of our lives. It is difficult to overstate the importance of living as the image bearers of God. Only by actually displaying the image of God can we be who our Creator intended us to be. Only by actually displaying the image of God can we offer the world around us the empirical evidence it wants for the truth of the gospel.

However, as God brings the reconciliation we have with him and with other believers into the reality of our day-to-day lives, we are forced to recognize that these reconciled relationships are imperfect. We have a foretaste of the complete renewal of the image of God, not its fulfillment. We are clouded mirrors of God's likeness, not clear ones. Perfection is not within our grasp, and will not be until the Lord returns.

Many Christians seem to think that when they come to faith, God should make them sinless, glorified creatures overnight. However, God has not chosen to work that way with us. Although in his sight we *are* changed from enemies into beloved children immediately, it takes a whole lifetime and more to bring our renewed relationship with him into every sphere of our lives.

In this sense, the Christian life is like learning to play a musical instrument. The day my wife decided to learn the guitar, she could truthfully say that she was a guitarist. But when I listened to her, and then listened to someone who had been playing for a number of years, I wasn't even sure they were playing the same instrument! My wife was truly a guitarist, but it was sometimes painful to listen to her broken, lifeless music. Now, several years later, it is a joy to hear her play. She is no more a guitarist than she was on the first day, but now she is an accomplished musician.

In the same way, we are truly complete Christians the very day we meet the Lord, yet it takes years to learn to walk with him. We can no more expect immediate perfection in the Christian life than my wife could expect to be a great guitarist the first time she picked up the instrument. She still makes mistakes, but they are far less frequent than when she began, and her music has, with the years, become quite beautiful. We can expect the same growth as we live more deeply in the Christian life.

As Christians, we have received a foretaste of the life of the new creation. As we continue to walk with God, we can see substantial, even if imperfect, renewal of the image of God in our present life. Walking in this substantial renewal of our relationships with God and with each other is our calling as Christians. As we walk in our re-creation, we can look forward to the time when our foretaste will become fulfillment. This is our "blessed hope, the appearing of the glory of our great God and Savior Jesus Christ" (Ti 2:13).

Image and Glory

There is one final aspect of our life as the worshipping community which we need to consider: the role we have as the "glory of God." This role is intimately related both to our day-to-day walk as image bearers in the present time and to the ultimate hope of our fulfilled renewal as his image when the Lord returns.

"Image" and "glory" occur together in several New Testament passages (Heb 1:3; 2 Cor 3:18), but the most troublesome and most instructive passage linking them is 1 Corinthians 11:7. The context of this verse is Paul's instructions about worship, specifically the relationship of a wife to her husband during worship. He says that wives should have their heads covered when praying or prophesying, but their husbands should not. The reason, he says, is that "A man ought not to cover his head, since he is the image *and glory* of God; but woman is the *glory* of man."

The first point about this verse is that the image of God and the glory of God are somehow connected, but also different. They are not just two ways of saying the same thing: The woman can be called the glory of man but never his image. She bears God's image, not her husband's. Notice also that Paul does not say that man "glorifies God," but rather that man *is* the glory of God. In understanding what the apostle means when he calls us "the glory of God" we shall see something about both the final outcome of bearing God's image and the way in which we walk as his image bearers in the present age.

The New Testament writers use the word "glory" (Greek, *doxa*) in several ways. We must determine the proper definition from the context when we attempt to understand Paul's intent in calling man the "glory of God."

One meaning "glory" often has in New Testament usage is that of "praise." This use of *doxa* gives us our English word "doxology." "Praise God from whom all blessings flow . . ." is a doxology because it sings praises to God. In Matthew we find an example of "glory" used to mean "praise." As a result of Jesus' great ministry to the sick, "the throng wondered, when they saw the dumb speaking, the maimed whole, the lame walking, and the blind seeing; and they glorified [praised] the God of Israel" (Mt 15:31; see also Mt 9:8, Mk 2:12, Lk 5:26-27, Rom 15:9, and Rv 16:9).

Another meaning of "glory," is "brilliance" or "radiance." This is the meaning which usually comes to mind when we think of the glory of God. In Acts 22:11, Paul, speaking to the Jews of his conversion on the Damascus Road says that Jesus appeared to him there in a brilliant light. "My companions led me by the hand into Damascus, because the *brilliance* [literally, *doxa*] of the light blinded me." This conception of glory as a bright light is a fairly common one in the Old Testament, especially in connection with the light of God's presence in the tabernacle (Ex 40:34-35).

This sense of "glory" as "brilliant light" is occasionally found in the New Testament as well, but light is only one part of the scripture's concept of glory. Blinding light is a physical manifestation of God's glory, not his glory itself. When Paul says we are "the glory of God," he does not mean that we light up. As C.S. Lewis commented, "Who wishes to become a kind of living electric light bulb?"

In 1 Corinthians 11:7, Paul uses "glory" in still another sense, one which is used with great frequency in the New Testament. We can see a glimpse of this particular usage in Paul's list in the first chapter of Ephesians of the blessings God has bestowed upon us.

> He predestined us to adoption as sons through Jesus Christ to himself, according to the kind intention of his will, *to the praise of the glory of his grace*, which he freely bestowed upon us in the Beloved. (Eph 1:5-6)

> In him, according to the purpose of him who accomplishes all things according to the counsel of his will, we who first hoped in Christ have been destined and appointed to live *for the praise of his glory*. (Eph 1:11-12)

> You were sealed with the promised Holy Spirit, which is the guarantee of our inheritance until we acquire possession of it, *to the praise of his glory*. (Eph 1:13b-14)

The phrase "to the praise of his glory" occurs only these three times in the entire New Testament. It is clearly not a way of saying either "to the praise of God's praise" or "to the praise of God's light." The two other meanings of "glory" mentioned previously simply do not fit Paul's usage here. When he says "to the praise of his glory," he seems to have something specific about God in mind.

In the Gospels, God's glory is often linked to his role as the one who judges all men. "For the Son of man is to come with his angels *in the glory of his Father*, and then he will repay every man for what he has done. Truly, I say to you, there are some standing here who will not taste death before they see the Son of man coming *in his kingdom*" (Mt 16:27-28).

Two things are worthy of note here. First, Jesus connects his glory with his role as judge (cf., Mt 25:31; Mk 8:38). Second, he parallels "glory" with "kingdom." In verse 27, the Son of Man is coming "in the *glory* of his Father" and in verse 28, he is coming "in his kingdom."

An even better example of the association of "glory" and "kingdom" occurs in an incident recorded by two of the gospels. James and John decided that they wanted the highest places in the kingdom. In order to make such a request seem a little less obnoxious, they had their mother ask Jesus on their behalf. Matthew records her request this way: "Command that these two sons of mine may sit, one at your right hand and one at your left, *in your kingdom*" (Mt 20:21). Mark puts the responsibility for the request directly on James and John and records it as "Grant us to sit, one at your right hand and one at your left, *in your glory*" (Mk 10:37).

Matthew says that the Apostles' request was to sit "in your *kingdom*" and Mark "in your *glory*." Both clearly intended to convey the same thought since they are telling the same incident. It seems that in this case "kingdom" and "glory" are virtual synonyms.

This explains the use of "glory" as a partner to "kingdom" and "judgment" in our other passages: God's glory *is* his kingly rule. This is Paul's meaning when he speaks of "the praise of his glory" in Ephesians 1. God is to be praised for the sovereignty and authority of his kingly rule—his glory. The Triune God is the sovereign Lord over the heavens and the earth, a just and mighty King. His authority and power as King are often referred to in scripture by the word "glory."

The fulfilled kingdom of God is metaphorically called "glory" for this very reason: God will have obvious kingly rule. "When Christ who is our life appears, then you also will appear with him *in glory*" (Col 3:4). Paul calls the coming kingdom "glory" because then God will objectively rule the earth and we will see his glory, his kingly rule, face to face.

However, the glory of God is not nonexistent now, only to be revealed when Christ returns. God's kingly rule is also manifest in the present order. Commenting on Jesus' first miracle, the changing of water to wine at Cana, John says, "This, the first of his signs, Jesus did at Cana in Galilee, and manifested *his glory* [in this case, his kingly rule over nature]; and his disciples believed in him" (Jn 2:11).

Some time later, Jesus came to the tomb of Lazarus, a man he loved deeply. He ordered the stone which covered the mouth of the crypt taken away. Lazarus' sister Martha replied to him " 'Lord, by this time there will be an odor, for he has been dead four days.' Jesus said to her, 'Did I not tell you that if you would believe you would see the glory of God?' " (Jn 11:39-40). Then Jesus commanded the dead Lazarus to come forth from his tomb, thereby displaying his glory, his kingly rule over death.

This revelation of his glory — his authority and power — was an integral part of Jesus' mission. He preached that the kingdom of God was at hand (Mt 4:17), but his preaching was not in words only. The gospels record that "He went about all Galilee, teaching in their synagogues and preaching the gospel of the kingdom *and* healing every disease and every infirmity among the people" (Mt 4:23). His proclamation of the kingdom included performing miracles, healing the sick, raising the dead, and casting out demons.

By these concrete demonstrations of his sovereignty over nature, the results of the fall, and the fallen angelic realm, Jesus proved that his glory, his kingly reign, was not only reserved for the future, but had entered the present age as well. The glory of God, as we see it in Jesus' ministry and the expectation of the coming of the kingdom, involves God's authority and powerful rule in both this age and the age to come.

Authority in the Church

Before applying this meaning of glory as God's kingly rule to the question of man's role as the "glory of God," we must consider a few aspects of the meaning of authority. Twentieth century men have an almost instinctive aversion to authority. There are many reasons for this aversion, but we as Christians must understand that the church was never intended to be an anarchy. One result of being filled with the Holy Spirit is an attitude and practice of submission to other believers (Eph 5:18-21).

To this end, Paul appointed elders in his churches (Acts 14:23) and commissioned his co-workers to do the same (Ti 1:5). Elders were to facilitate the submission to one another which results from the Spirit's ministry. They were, in a sense, rulers of the church under God (1 Tm 5:17). They were carefully to shepherd the people whom God put in their charge (Acts 20:28). For their part, the people of God were implicitly expected to respond to their shepherding authority (Heb 13:17).

The scriptures teach about the value of spiritual authority, but we often balk at the idea of such authority in the church. One reason why we do so is because we transfer the world's concept of authority into Christianity. Jesus expressly taught against such a transfer when he settled a fight among his disciples about who would be the greatest in the coming kingdom. Jesus' response to the dispute brings out the radical difference between authority in the world and authority in the kingdom of God. "The kings of the Gentiles exercise lordship over them; and those in authority over them are called benefactors. *But not so with you*; rather let the greatest among you become as the youngest, and the leader as one who serves" (Lk 22:25-26).

Authority in God's kingdom is based on "serving," not on "lording." The shepherd of a flock does not beat his sheep, but serves them and, if necessary, lays down his life for them. He has the authority toward them and they respond willingly to him. Jesus himself set the example for this kind of serving authority:

> *Have this mind among yourselves, which you have in Christ Jesus*, who, though he was in the form of God, did not count equality with God a thing to be grasped, but emptied himself, *taking the form of a servant*, being born in the likeness of men. And being found in human form he humbled himself and became obedient unto death, even death on a cross. *Therefore God has highly exalted him*. (Phil 2:5-9)

Jesus, as head of the church, is the greatest servant of all. He has authority toward the church, but the result of that authority is serving, not lording. The analogy of Christ's authority toward his church with the authority of a husband toward his wife is explicitly carried out in Ephesians 5:22-23. "For the husband is the head of the wife as Christ is the head of the church" (v. 23). Paul's emphasis here is primarily on the serving nature of the husband's headship, and only secondarily on the wife's response to his headship.

The issue here is not one of superiority of men over women or of husbands over wives; as far as God is concerned there is neither "male nor female; for you are all one in Christ Jesus" (Gal 3:28). The husband is to grant his wife "honor as a fellow-heir of the grace of life" (1 Pt 3:7). Rather, the issue of authority is the service of love which the husband is to offer to his wife.

Man as God's Glory

Now we are ready to consider Paul's description of man as "the image and glory of God" in 1 Corinthians 11. His argument here refers to the same type of headship of husband toward wife which we saw in Ephesians 5. To make sure his readers do not infer from this that husbands are superior to wives, he extends the concept into the Godhead. "But I want you to understand that the head of every man is Christ, the head of a woman is her husband, the head of Christ is God" (1 Cor 11:3). Of course the Son is inferior to the Father in *no respect whatsoever*. Nevertheless, he voluntarily submitted to the Father's headship, his service of love.

Because the Trinity itself manifests relationships of headship, the service of headship can neither be ignored as irrelevant nor thought of as evil. Christ, "very God of very God" as the creed says, equal with the Father in all respects, submits himself to the headship of the Father. In a like manner, the wife, fully and equally co-heir of Christ with her husband, should submit herself to his service of love. The husband should offer this service even to extent of dying for his wife.

This concept of headship in equality is the basis for Paul's answer to the Corinthians' question about the specific cultural expression of wives covering their heads during worship. Theories abound in the scholarly literature about what the customary procedure in Corinth was and where they got it. However, it seems clear that in some way a head covering in Corinth symbolized the headship of the husband toward his wife (1 Cor 11:10).

The substance of Paul's teaching on this point is to urge the Corinthians to be consistent in this practice even while women were praying or prophesying. Even though a wife may enter into ministry (here, by prayer or prophesying) on an equal basis with her husband, she is still to acknowledge her husband's service of love for her. Thus he argues that even when a wife prophesies, speaking directly from God who is her ultimate head, she should acknowledge the earthly headship of her husband. In this case, she acknowledges this through wearing a head covering.

Then Paul says, "A man ought not to cover his head, since he is the image *and glory* of God; but woman [his wife] is *the glory* of man" (1 Cor 11:7). How is a wife "the glory" of her husband? She is his glory as she acts in response to his service of love. If we are *very* careful to distinguish Christian authority from the pagan concept of authority as "lording," we can say that this service of love which headship entails is the Christian counterpart to "kingly rule." God's kingly rule over the whole creation is not a "lording" but a service of love. So too the husband's headship with respect to his wife is to be like God's kingly rule, his service of love. The wife is to act as his glory in her response to this service of love.

This is precisely how the concepts of headship and submission are worked out in Ephesians 5. The husband, as head, is not to make his wife into his maid or his lacky. As head, he is called to a service of love which requires that he pour himself out for his wife, even if it means his death (Eph 5:25). Christ is the example of this—he died for us. In his headship toward the church, his kingly rule and his self-giving service of love coincide. They are only two ways of saying the same thing.

How then does the husband act as the glory of God? The reason is the same: He is the glory of God as he acts in response to God's service of love, that is, under his kingly rule.

We can extend Paul's specific statement about husbands to

include both men and women. All who have been made members of God's family and kingdom, who are "co-heirs of the grace of life," are called to act as the glory of God. Not only are we renewed to the image of God by the new birth, but we are also re-made into the glory of God. We are the glory of God because we are his people who respond to his service of love, his headship in our lives.

Man's problem from the outset has been his refusal to be the glory of God, to act under his headship. As we saw earlier, the sin of Adam and Eve was ultimately independence. Concerning the tree the serpent said, "For God knows that when you eat of it your eyes will be opened, and you will be like God, knowing good and evil" (Gn 3:5). By eating from the tree, Adam and Eve re-belled against the express command of God. They chose to be their own kings (being like God) rather than acknowledging God as king and living under his headship. Not only were the vertical and horizontal relationships of the image of God horribly dese-crated by the fall, but at the same time, mankind deliberately chose not to be the glory of God.

This is the essence of Paul's condemnation of mankind in Romans 3. He quotes the psalms and prophets in verses 10-16, detailing the pitiable condition of fallen man's relationships with God ("No one seeks for God;" "There is no fear of God before their eyes") and with other men ("They use their tongues to deceive," "Their feet are swift to shed blood," "The way of peace they do not know"). Paul sums it up in verse 23 when he says "all have sinned and fall short of *the glory of God.*" His point is not that man fails to light up like a light bulb, but that rebellious, fallen man does not act under the kingly rule of God. Thus he falls short of being God's glory.

As we become God's children by faith, we re-enter the sphere of God's kingly rule. Not only is his image which we bear renewed, but the glory of God is renewed as well. Consider the very fact that we can now address God as "Father." The term em-phasizes both the intimate relationship we now have with him, and the headship he exercises toward us as a father toward his children.

Our call as the glory of God will come to fruition when the

Lord Jesus returns to fulfill his kingdom. However, our role as the glory of God is renewed now, just as our role as the image of God is renewed. We already live under God's kingly rule, not just as a future expectation but also as a substantial reality in the present. Through the work of Christ, the new creation has broken into the present age. And we, as the re-created image bearers of God, are called to live in submission to his headship in the present age as well as in the age to come.

Reigning in Glory

Our life as the glory of God involves placing ourselves under God's kingly rule and receiving his service of love. Only as we do this can we fulfill our heavenly calling to be his image bearers. It is nonsense to try to bear God's image from a wholly human reference point. All our attempts at community with other men or communion with God are doomed to failure if they are merely our good ideas or dreams based on our fallen inabilities.

Instead, the healing of our damaged horizontal and vertical relationships must be energized and directed by the Triune God, so that we act under his kingly rule. It is impossible to truly act as "one body" unless we are "one body *in Christ*" in which each member looks to him as Lord for direction. Community will always be an unrealized ideal unless it is "the fellowship of the Holy Spirit" springing from the Godhead as its source and implemented, not originated, by us. Similarly, a life of intimate fellowship with God as his children and as worshippers is out of our reach apart from the continual ministry of the Holy Spirit. He is the one who must intercede for us in prayer (Rom 8:26-27) and remind us moment by moment that we are children of God (Rom 8:15-16). Thus, restoration of both the vertical and horizontal aspects of the image of God are practical only as we place ourselves under God's rule. If we refuse to be the glory of God, under his headship, the present reality of being his image bearers will be impossible. However, under God's kingly rule, our shattered relationships in the present life will be substantially reconciled and we can have hope for their complete renewal when the Lord Jesus returns.

Our role as the glory of God includes the notion of reigning in glory ourselves. The New Testament teaches that believers, as children of God the king, would reign with him in his kingdom. Paul says, "The saying is sure: If we have died with him, we shall also live with him; if we endure, we shall also reign with him" (2 Tm 2:11-12).

This is the thought in Romans 8:16-17, "The Spirit himself testifies with our spirit that we are God's children. Now if we are children, then we are heirs, heirs of God and *co-heirs* with Christ, if indeed we share in his sufferings in order that we may also share *in his glory*." Since we are made God's children in our new birth, it is obvious that we are then heirs of his kingdom. Because of our call to sonship, we are inheritors of God's kingdom with Christ, the only begotten Son. As sons and heirs, we are not only the glory of God, those who live under his rule, but we are ourselves glorified and will rule with him.

As we reign under God's reign in his eternal kingdom, he will have accomplished a complete renewal of the devastation of the fall. The scriptures record for us only two verbal communications from God to man before the fall. There were certainly many more than these two, but that the author of Genesis singled these out is significant. Both the communications are commands, and man broke both of them.

The first communication is in Genesis 1:28-30. Immediately after the creation of man, God commands Adam and Eve to rule over all the earth saying, "Be fruitful and multiply, and fill the earth and subdue it; and have dominion over the fish of the sea and over the birds of the air and over every living thing that moves upon the earth." As God's image bearers, Adam and Eve were given authority to rule over the earth as God's governors. They were told to reign under God not as puppets, but as true rulers exercising true kingly rule and serving the creation in love. Mankind's call as God's image bearer resulted in its call to be glorified, to reign over the earth.

The second time God speaks to man it is again in a command. "You may freely eat of every tree of the garden; but of the tree of the knowledge of good and evil you shall not eat, for in the day that you eat of it you shall die" (Gn 2:16-17). Here, God's command does not refer to the glorification of man as ruler over creation, but is a point of specific testing concerning his role as the glory of God living under God's reign. The essence of God's second directive to man is, "Respond to my kingly rule — continue to live as my glory."

At the fall, Adam and Eve broke both these commands. By eating of the tree, they refused to live under God's reign, choosing their own egotistic reign instead. As a result, the creation was cursed, bringing forth "thorns and thistles" in rebellion against man's headship (Gn 3:17-19). Man chose not to be God's glory, so he was no longer glorified.

Both these consequences of the fall will be erased in the new creation. Then we will live under God's reign as his glory, and we will reign as his children, as glorified fellow heirs with Christ. Then, in eternity, we will be completely remade into the image and glory of God.

The total renewal of man in eternity is the completion of what God has already begun in time. That which we have in foretaste now will then be expanded to include the remaking of our bodies and the renewal of the cursed creation. Paul draws this together as he speaks of our inheritance with Christ:

> I consider that the sufferings of this present time are not worth comparing with *the glory* that is to be revealed to us. For the creation waits with eager longing for the revealing of the sons of God; for the creation was subjected to futility, not of its own will but by the will of him who subjected it in hope; *because the creation itself will be set free* from its bondage to decay *and obtain the glorious liberty of the children of God.* (Rom 8:18-21)

When Christ returns to complete our renewal, the creation will be set free into the freedom of our reign, "the glorious liberty of the children of God," and the curse on it will be no more (Rv 22:3). For this the creation awaits our headship, our service of love.

In the eternal kingdom of God we will, with our renewed bodies in a new creation, display the image of God. Even now, as we await the fulfillment, we should see substantial renewal of God's glory, our life under his kingly rule. Our hope as God's image and glory is also to be our way of life. The Lord's command was to "let your light so shine before men, that they may see your good works and give glory to your Father who is in heaven" (Mt 5:16). The world should be able to see beauty in our interpersonal relationships and beauty in our relationship with God.

Because our hope is also to be our way of life, we are called to live out our future state in foretaste in the present. Our life as "the image and glory of God" will be imperfect because our hope lies in the future, not the present. Yet we will be really, substantially conformed to God's image and glory even in the present. Paul speaks to the living reality of our hope, telling us "to live sober, upright, and godly lives in this world [as our life now], awaiting our blessed hope, the appearing of the glory of our great God and Savior Jesus Christ" (Ti 2:12-13). This is the essence of the Christian understanding of man: His true being is a hope in the future that is lived out—not completely, but yet substantially—in the present.

Living out the foretaste of our hope will have two results. First, it will give the necessary empirical support to the gospel of Jesus Christ, so that when anyone asks, we can "give reason for the hope" that we have (1 Pt 3:15). Our life is an essential part of the ministry of reconciliation given to us.

Second, as we see substantial renewal of the image and glory of God in our lives in the present, we should long even more for the return of the Lord to complete that renewal. The more we taste the foretaste, the more we will hunger for the fullness waiting for us at the return of Christ. As we live out our hope as our way of life, we will be able to say eagerly with John "Amen. Come Lord Jesus" (Rv 22:20).

INDEX TO SCRIPTURE CITATIONS

INDEX